MUHAMMAD ALI

RINGSIDE

MUHAMMAD ALI
RINGSIDE

Compiled and Edited by John Miller & Aaron Kenedi

Introduction by James Earl Jones

A Bulfinch Press Book

Little, Brown and Company

Boston • New York • London

First Edition
ISBN 0-8212-2626-6
Library of Congress Catalog Card Number 99-72454

Bulfinch Press is an imprint and trademark of Little, Brown and Company (Inc.)

Quotes from Muhammad Ali: His Life and Times by Thomas Hauser reprinted with the permission of Simon & Schuster. Copyright ©1991 by Thomas Hauser and Muhammad Ali.

A portion of the proceeds from Muhammad Ali: Ringside will be donated to the National Parkinson's Foundation.

Design: Big Fish, San Francisco
Research: Eleanor Reagh
Copy editing: Pat Tompkins
Special thanks to Amy Rennert and Karen Dane

PRINTED IN HONG KONG

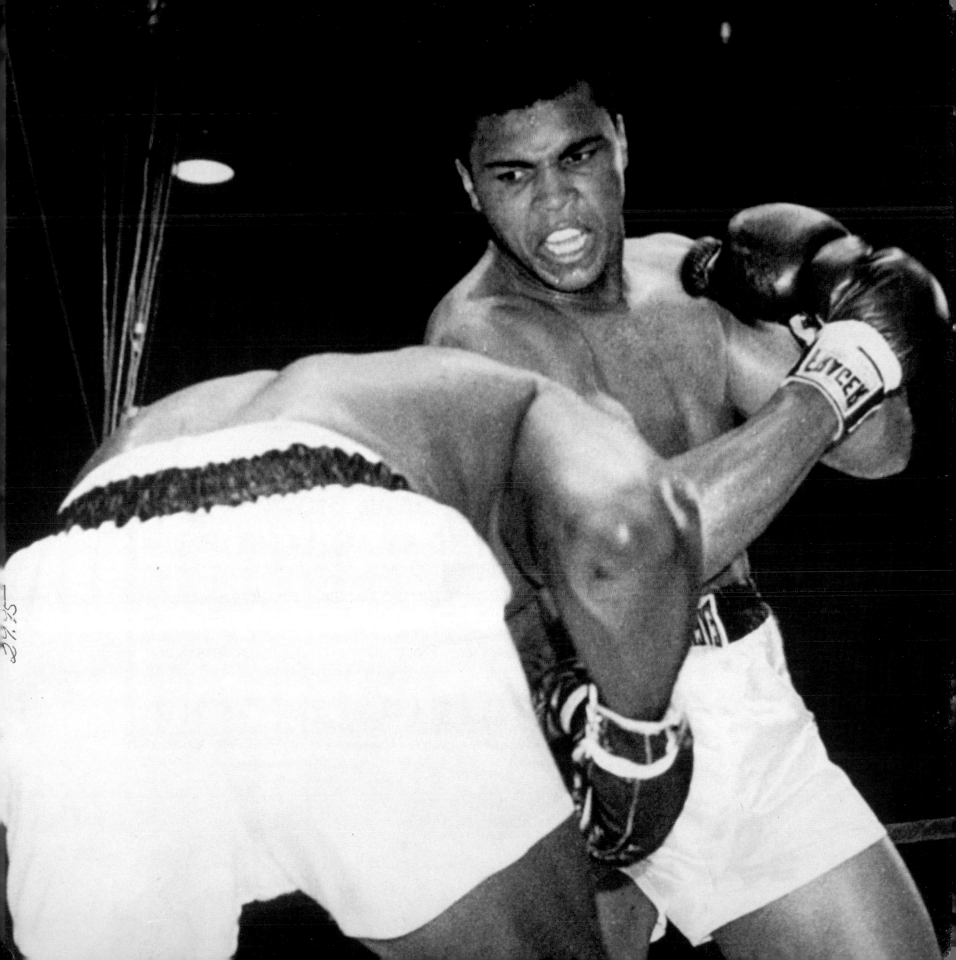

Contents

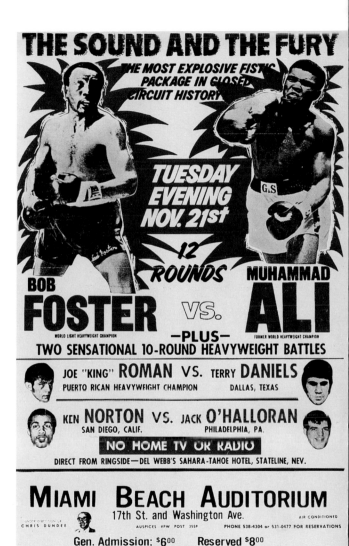

Introduction

by James Earl Jones

Muhammad Ali

has been called a hero, an American icon, a spiritual ambassador, a consummate showman and entertainer, and a "heavyweight Fred Astaire." He did indeed move like a dancer in the ring, jousting with dazzling power and grace. To watch Muhammad Ali at ringside or on film is to behold grace in motion. To come to know him as a person is to discover the interior grace of a brave man now at peace with himself and the world.

I met Muhammad Ali in 1968, four years after he was crowned heavyweight champion. The warrior was taking his stand against war, refusing induction in the Army, already paying a dear price for his act of conscience. I was appearing in *The Great White Hope* on Broadway, playing Jack Jefferson, a character based on Jack Johnson, the controversial heavyweight champion who won his title in 1908. In 1913 Johnson fled the country after a love affair led to his conviction for violating the Mann Act—transporting a woman across state lines for "immoral purposes."

One night after a performance of *The Great White Hope*, Ali came backstage to my dressing room.

"James," he said, "go out in the auditorium."

Curious, I did what he asked. Ali stood on the stage in the dark, empty auditorium and spoke one of the lines from our play, as if he were Jack Johnson: "Here I is. Here I is."

Then he turned to me. "How was that?"

"Ali, that was great," I told him.

"Not only great," he said. "This is my story. You replace the issue of white women with the issues of religion and the war, and this is my story."

That began our friendship.

Once during the filming of *The Great White Hope* in Hollywood, Ali and I put on boxing gloves for a promotional stunt. Imagine standing there, glove to glove with the great Muhammad Ali.

"Go on," he kept saying, dancing that famous dance of his. "Hit me. Hit me."

When I did not respond, he egged me on, that twinkle in his eye. "Hit me, brother, hit me."

Finally, I drew back and gave him my best. That handsome face hardly moved. Those eyes kept twinkling. Those feet kept dancing. I did not faze the champ.

He never laid a hand on me, but in the simple act of blocking my blow, Ali broke my thumb.

This self-made man is endowed with superb gifts that reach beyond his athletic power and prowess. His charisma compels fans worldwide. The Ali mystique is part Kentucky grit, part inner fire, part magic, part show biz, part sheer will, forged in hard times and courage. There is a deep spiritual core to the man that empowers and illuminates his work and his legacy. Gutsy determination and discipline defined him as a champion. These traits are stronger that ever today as Ali copes with the physical limitations of Parkinson's syndrome.

In July of 1992, Ali flew into Los Angeles to receive the Jim Thorpe Lifetime Achievement Award. I was present that night for the Jim Thorpe Pro Sports Awards Show. Several boxing champions were there, black and white, newcomers as well as old timers, including Floyd Patterson, George Foreman, and Evander Holyfield. Each stood in his own personal light, with center stage reserved for Ali.

To a person, the audience stood in tribute as he approached his spotlight. Then he took the microphone to speak. Gone are the days of the exuberant poetry with which he used to taunt his opponents. We waited to see what he would say, what he could say.

Ali spoke slowly and softly. He had flown in all the way from China for that evening, he told us. He had traveled a great distance, through several time zones. It had not been easy to get here. We listened quietly, sympathetically, hanging on his words.

And then Ali paused, held his trophy aloft, and said with a mischievous smile: "I go to all that trouble, and this is all I get?"

The Champ brought down the house, and showed us, if we had any doubt, that the inner Ali is intact, the fires still burn, the lionhearted spirit is undaunted.

It is not by trophies and records that I know my friend Muhammad Ali; not by accolades and triumphs in the ring, or controversy outside it. It is by his extraordinary beauty and grace as an athlete, and the even more durable beauty and grace of his spirit as a human being.

You can easily forgive a man like that for breaking your thumb.

—JAMES EARL JONES
April 7, 1999

"I dream I'm running down Broad-way. That's the main street in Louisville, and all of the sudden there's a truck coming at me. I run at the truck and I wave my arms, and then I take off and I'm flying. I go right up over the truck, and all the people are standing around and cheering and waving at me. And I wave back and I keep on flying. I dream that dream all of the time."

—Cassius Clay

1960s

by Alex Haley

The Chicago Tribune Charities, Inc.
PRESENTS THE
32nd Annual Golden Gloves Finals
SANCTIONED BY CENTRAL A. A. U.   CHICAGO STADIUM
Official Program 35c   March 11, 1959

When Cassius Clay was a baby, he was called "GG," as he constantly babbled "g,g,g." After winning his first title, the 1959 Golden Gloves, he explained: "You know what I meant? I was trying to say Golden Gloves."

Clay vs. Liston:
Birth of a Legend

It wasn't until 9:55 on a
night last February that anyone began to take seriously the extravagant boasts of Cassius Marcellus Clay: That was the moment when the redoubtable Sonny Liston, sitting dazed and disbelieving on a stool in Miami Beach's Convention Hall, resignedly spat out his mouthpiece—and relinquished the world's heavyweight boxing championship to the brash young braggart whom he, along with the nation's sportswriters and nearly everyone else, had dismissed as a loudmouthed pushover.

Leaping around the ring in a frenzy of glee, Clay screamed, "I am the greatest! I am the king!"—the strident rallying cry of a campaign of self-celebration, punctuated with rhyming couplets predicting victory, which had rocketed him from relative obscurity as a 1960 Olympic Gold Medal winner to dubious renown as the "villain" of a title match with the

> **"Clay is not a fake, and even his blustering and playground poetry are valid; they demonstrate that a new and more complicated generation has moved onto the scene.... Clay is definitely my man."**
> —LeRoi Jones

To complete his amateur boxing career, Clay represented the United States in the 1960 Olympics in Rome. He returned home a hero, bringing back a gold medal and a poem: "To make America the greatest is my goal / So I beat the Russian, and I beat the Pole / And for the USA won the Medal of Gold."

least lovable heavyweight champion in boxing history. Undefeated in 100 amateur fights and all 19 professional bouts, the cocky 22-year-old had become, if not another Joe Louis, at least the world's wealthiest poet (with a purse of $600,000), and one of its most flamboyant public figures.

Within 24 hours of his victory, he also became sports' most controversial cause célèbre when he announced at a press conference that he was henceforth to be billed on fight programs only as Muhammad Ali, his new name as a full-fledged member of the Black Muslims, the militant nation-wide Negro religious cult that preaches racial segregation, black supremacy and unconcealed hostility toward whites....

We approached the mercurial Muslim with our request for a searching interview about his fame, his heavyweight crown and his faith. Readily consenting, he invited us to join him... in his chauffeured, air-conditioned Cadillac limousine on leisurely drives through Harlem. We interjected our questions as the opportunities presented themselves—between waves and shouts exchanged by the champion and ogling pedestrians, and usually over the din of the limousine's dashboard phonograph, blaring Clay's recording of "I Am the Greatest." We began the conversation on our own blaring note.

HALEY Are you really the loudmouthed exhibitionist you seem to be, or is it all for the sake of publicity?
CLAY I been attracting attention ever since I been able to walk and talk. When I was just a little boy in school, I caught onto how nearly everybody likes to watch somebody that acts different. Like, I wouldn't ride the school bus, I would *run* to school alongside it, and all the kids would be waving and hollering at me and calling me nuts. It made me somebody special. Or at recess time, I'd start a fight with somebody to draw a crowd. I always liked drawing crowds. When I started fighting serious, I found out that grown people, the fight fans, acted just like those school kids. Almost from my first fights, I'd bigmouth to anybody who would listen about what I was going to do to whoever I was going to fight, and people would

SEE HEAVYWEIGHT FISTIC DYNAMITE EXPLODE

MAD. SQ. GARDEN

8th AVE., 49th - 50th STS.

SAT. FEB. 10 • 8:30 P.M.

MAIN EVENT — 10 ROUNDS

CASSIUS CLAY

Undefeated As A Pro. The Most Talked About Heavyweight in Boxing Today. 1960 Olympic Champion

VS

SONNY K. O. BANKS

Detroit's New Young Joe Louis. Scored 9 Knockouts in 12 Fights.

OT E E EAT FI TS

RESERVED SEATS $2 - $3 - $4 - $6 & $8 Incl. Tax

TICKETS NOW ON SALE AT BOX OFFICE - Phone CO 5-6815

Clay's first major professional fight was against Sonny Banks at Madison Square Garden in 1962. He predicted a victory, claiming that "to beat me, you got to be greater than great." Clay finished Banks in the fourth round.

FREE PARKING REAR OF AUDITORIUM!
PARQUEO GRATIS EN LA ZONA DETRAS DEL AUDITORIUM!

★ # BOXING ★

MIAMI BEACH
CONVENTION HALL

UNDER DIRECTION OF
CHRIS DUNDEE
AUSPICES
VFW Post 3559

17th St. and Washington Ave.

AIR CONDITIONED

Ph. JE. 1-0477 • JE. 2-3329 • JE. 8-4304 · For Reservations

WEDNESDAY FEB. 28th 8:45 P.M.

·CLAY·

10-ROUNDS-10
'HEAVYWEIGHTS'

CASSIUS
CLAY

"The Talk of the Country"

vs.

·WARNER·

DON
WARNER

PHILA.
"K.O." ARTIST

GENERAL ADM. $1.50   **RESERVED** $2.50 - $3.50   **RINGSIDE** $5.00

In 1962, Clay—now known as The Louisville Lip—won six more fights, predicting not only victory, but the knock out round. Sure enough, Sonny Banks fell in four; Lavorante went down in five. The only one Clay misfired on was Don Warner, who he KO'd in the fourth, instead of the promised fifth. He explained: "I had to. He refused to shake my hand at the opening bell."

Mouthwise, Clay met his match against Archie Moore in 1962. The fight was stopped in the fourth. Clay was the victor.

"Why doesn't somebody just get that old guy a pension; why doesn't somebody just retire him? . . . When you come to the fight don't block the door, 'cause you'll all go home after round four." —Cassius Clay

"The only way I'll fall in four is by toppling over Clay's prostrate form. . . . Clay can go with speed in all directions, including straight down if hit properly. I have a good solid right hand that will fit nicely on his chops." —Archie Moore

go out of their way to come and see, hoping I would get beat. When I wasn't no more than a kid fighter, they would put me on bills because I was a drawing card, because I run my mouth so much. Other kids could battle and get all bloody and lose or win and didn't hardly nobody care, it seemed like, except maybe their families and their buddies. But the minute I would come in sight, the people would start to hollering "Bash in his nose!" or "Button his fat lip!" or something like that. You would have thought I was some well-known pro ten years older than I was. But I didn't care what they said, long as they kept coming to see me fight. They paid their money, they was entitled to a little fun.

HALEY How did your first fight come about?

CLAY Well, on my twelfth birthday, I got a new bicycle as a present from my folks, and I rode it to a fair that was being held at the Columbia Gymnasium, and when I come out, my bike was gone. I was so mad I was crying, and a policeman, Joe Martin, come up and I told him I was going to whip whoever took my bike. He said I ought to take some boxing lessons to learn how to whip the thief better, and I did. That's when I started fighting. Six weeks later, I won my first fight over another boy twelve years old, a white boy. And in a year I was fighting on TV. Joe Martin advised me against trying to just fight my way up in clubs and preliminaries, which could take years and maybe get me all beat up. He said I ought to try the Olympics, and if I won, that would give me automatically a number-ten pro rating. And that's just what I did. . . .

HALEY Your poetry has been described by many critics as "horrible." Do you think it is?

CLAY I bet my poetry gets printed and quoted more than any that's turned out by the poem writers that them critics like. I don't pay no attention to no kind of critics about nothing. If they knew as much as they claim to about what they're criticizing, they ought to be doing that instead of just standing on the side lines using their mouth.

Souvenir Program   25c

Olympic Boxing Club Promotion
PRESENTED BY
CAL EATON and GEORGE PARNASSUS

World Heavyweight Title Elimination

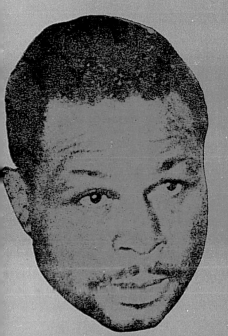

Archie
MOORE
WORLD'S LIGHT HEAVYWEIGHT CHAMPION

vs.

Cassius
CLAY
TOP RANKING HEAVYWEIGHT CONTENDER

L.A. SPORTS ARENA — THURSDAY NIGHT, NOV. 15, 1962

EMPIRE STADIUM ✦ TUESDAY
WEMBLEY
18th JUNE 1963

JACK SOLOMONS proudly presents

DOORS OPEN 5.30

THE WORLD'S GREATEST SHOWMAN AND PERSONALITY—CASSIUS CLAY
"THE LOUISVILLE LIP"   "CASSIUS THE GREAT"

COMMENCE 7.30 P.M.

ELIMINATING CONTEST FOR THE HEAVYWEIGHT CHAMPIONSHIP OF THE WORLD
10 x 3 MINUTE ROUNDS
"THE FABULOUS"

Clay K.O.'s Archie Moore

CASSIUS CLAY

U.S.A.   WORLD'S No. 3 HEAVYWEIGHT CONTENDER
Sensational fast talking and fast punching undefeated young heavyweight. The world's greatest personality

v   "OUR 'ENERY"

HENRY COOPER

ENGLAND.   WORLD'S No. 6 HEAVYWEIGHT CONTENDER.   With the best straight left and left hook in the world

Cooper K.O.'s Dick Richardson

SAYS CASSIUS MARCIUS CLAY:
I'M THE GREATEST FIGHTER IN THE WORLD   I'M THE GREATEST POET IN THE WORLD
I'M THE GREATEST PREDICTOR IN THE WORLD   I'M THE NEXT CHAMPION OF THE WORLD

WATCH PRESS AND POSTERS FOR SENSATIONAL SUPPORTING BOUTS FOR THIS NIGHT OF ALL NIGHTS

BOOK YOUR SEATS IMMEDIATELY AND NO INCREASE IN PRICES FOR THIS FABULOUS SHOW

12/6   25/-   £2.2.0   £3.3.0   £4.4.0   and £6.6.0

Obtainable from :   Jack Solomons, 41 Gt. Windmill Street, W.1. Ger 9195/6. Wembley Stadium, Wembley 1234. Thomas A'Beckett, 320 Old Kent Road, S.E.1. ROD 7334. Alf Mancini, "Rifle", 80 Fulham Palace Road, W.6. RIV 6502. Len Mancini, "Lord Palmerston", 648 King's Road, S.W.6. REN 4501. Jim Smith, 102 Ophir Road, Northend, Portsmouth 63132. H. Gorman, 9 Lynton Place, Rumney, Cardiff. Lew Phillips, 177 Corporation Street, Birmingham. CEN 3652. Jim Wicks, 139 Footscray Road, Eltham, S.E.9. Eltham 5254. Alex Griffiths, Deauville, Dingle Lane, Willenhall. Staffs., and usual Agents

WILLSONS (PRINTERS) LTD. LEICESTER PHONE 21210

HALEY How often have you been right in predicting the round of a knockout?

CLAY I ain't missed but twice. If you figure out the man you're up against, and you know what you can do, then you can pretty much do it whenever you get ready. Once I call the round, I plan what I'm going to do in the fight. Like, you take Archie Moore. He's a better fighter than Sonny Liston. He's harder to hit, the way he bobs and weaves, and he's smart. You get careless and he'll drop you. I guess he knows more tricks in the ring than anybody but Sugar Ray. But he was fat and forty-five, and he had to be looking for a lucky punch before he got tired. I just had to pace myself so as to tire him. I hooked and jabbed him silly the first round, then I coasted the second. Right at the end of the second, he caught me with a good right on the jaw, but it didn't do me no harm. Then I started out the third throwing leather on him, and when I could feel him wearing down, I slowed up, looking for my spots to hit him. And then in the fourth round, when I had said he was going down, I poured it on him again. And he did go down; he was nearly out. But he got up at eight. A few combinations sent him back down, and then the referee stopped it. It was just like I planned.

HALEY After you had scored victories over Archie Moore, Charley Powell, Doug Jones and Henry Cooper, how did you go about your campaign to get a match with Liston?

CLAY Well, the big thing I did is that until then, I had just been loudmouthing mostly for the *public* to hear me, to build up gates for my fights. I hadn't never been messing personally with whoever I was going to fight—and that's what I started when it was time to go after Liston. I had been studying Liston careful, all along, ever since he had come up in the rankings, and Patterson was trying to duck him. You know what Patterson was saying—that Liston had such a bad police record, and prison record and all that. He wouldn't be a good example for boxing like Patterson would—the pure, clean-cut American boy.

JACK SOLOMONS presents an
Eliminating Contest for the
HEAVYWEIGHT CHAMPIONSHIP OF THE WORLD
Wembley Stadium
Tuesday 18th June, 1963

OFFICIAL PROGRAMME TWO SHILLINGS & SIXPENCE

Cassius Clay   Henry Cooper

Clay's last tune-up fight for Liston matched him against British champ Henry Cooper. Clay's call: "After five rounds Henry Cooper will think his name is [astronaut] Gordon Cooper. He'll be in orbit!" Cooper was a TKO in five.

The biggest challenge of Clay's early career came against the ferocious Sonny Liston. Clay wasn't intimidated: "I'm handsome, I'm fast, I can't possibly be beat. I'm ready to go to war now. If I see that bear on the street, I'll beat him before the fight. I'll beat him like I'm his

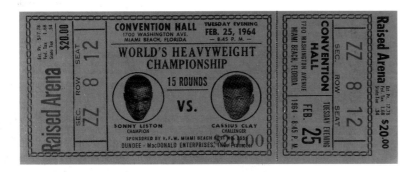

daddy.... I'm going to put that ugly bear on the floor, and after the fight I'm going to build myself a pretty home and use him as a bearskin rug.... Liston even smells like a bear.... He's too ugly to be the world champ. The world's champ should be pretty like me."

HALEY You were saying you had been studying Liston....
CLAY I don't see no harm in telling it now. The first time, it was right after Liston had bought his new home in Denver, and my buddies and me was driving from Los Angeles to New York in my bus. This was Archie Robinson, who takes care of business for me, and Howard Bingham, the photographer, and some more buddies. I had bought this used thirty-passenger bus, a 1953 Flexible—you know, the kind you see around airports. We had painted it red and white with WORLD'S MOST COLORFUL FIGHTER across the top. Then I had LISTON MUST GO IN EIGHT painted across the side right after Liston took the title. We had been driving around Los Angeles, and up and down the freeways in the bus, blowing the horn, "Oink! Oink! Oink!" drawing people's attention to me. When I say I'm colorful, I believe in *being* colorful. Anyway, this time, when we started out for New York, we decided it would be a good time to pay Liston a visit at his new house.

We had the address from the newspapers, and we pulled up in his front yard in the bus about three o'clock in the morning and started blowing: "*Oink! Oink! Oink! Oink!*" In other houses, lights went on and windows went up. You know how them white people felt about that black man just moved in there anyway, and we sure wasn't helping it none. People was hollering things, and we got out with the headlights blazing and went up to Liston's door, just about as Liston got there. He had on nylon shorty pajamas. And he was mad. He first recognized Howard Bingham, the photographer, whom he had seen in Los Angeles. "What you want, black mother?" he said to Howard. I was standing right behind Howard, flinging my cane back and forth in the headlights, hollering loud enough for everybody in a mile to hear me, "Come on out of there! I'm going to whip you right now! Come on out of there and protect your home! If you don't

> "It's my time to howl/ rumble, man, rumble/ float like a butterfly/ sting like a bee/ your hands can't hit what your eyes can't see."
>
> —Cassius Clay

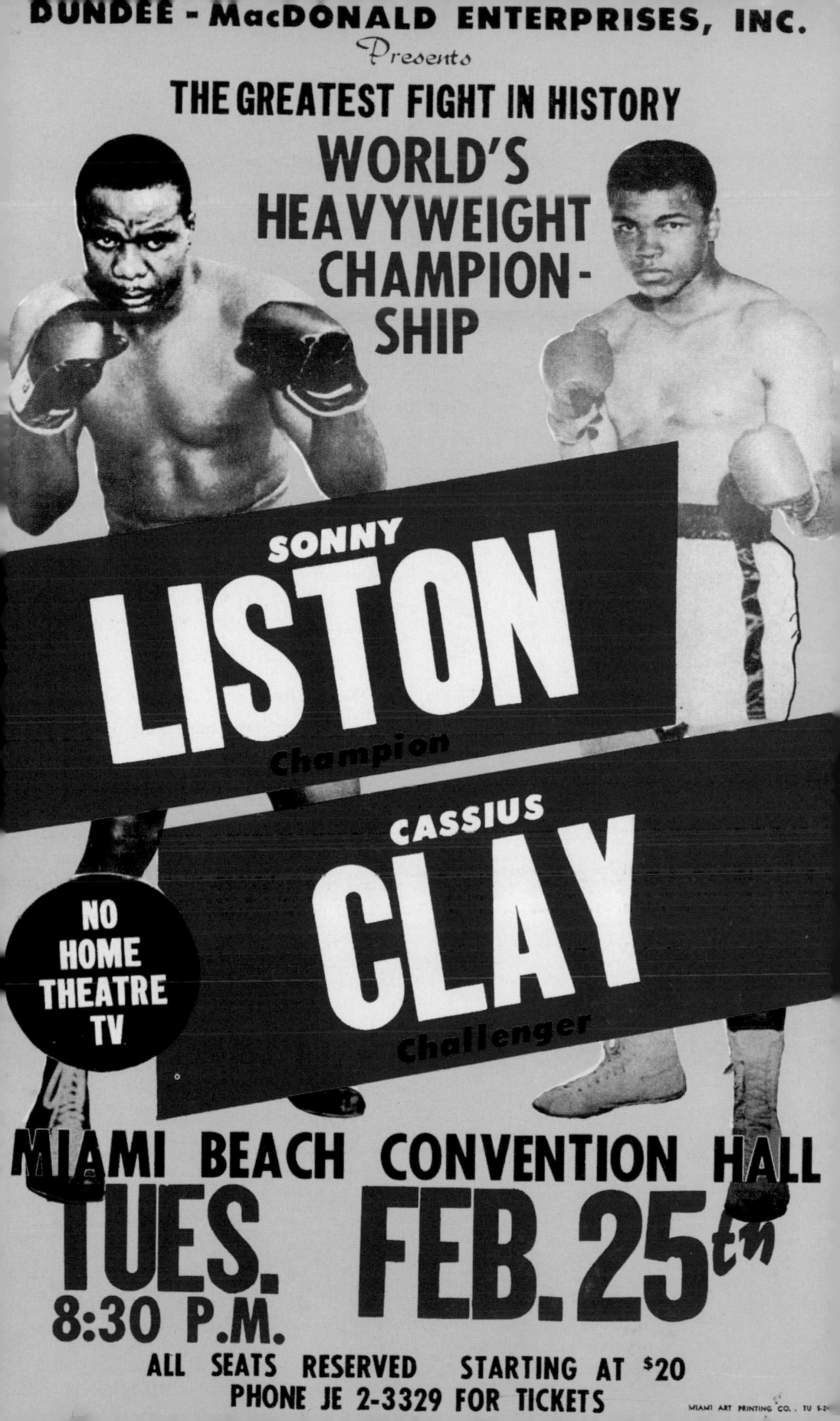
DUNDEE - MacDONALD ENTERPRISES, INC.
Presents
THE GREATEST FIGHT IN HISTORY
WORLD'S HEAVYWEIGHT CHAMPION-SHIP
SONNY
LISTON
Champion
CASSIUS
CLAY
Challenger
NO HOME THEATRE TV
MIAMI BEACH CONVENTION HALL
TUES.
8:30 P.M.
FEB. 25th
ALL SEATS RESERVED STARTING AT $20
PHONE JE 2-3329 FOR TICKETS
MIAMI ART PRINTING CO.

Not many gave Clay a chance against the fearsome Liston. Forty-three of forty-six boxing writers polled thought Liston would win.

"The loudmouth from Louisville is likely to have a lot of vainglorious boasts jammed down his throat by a ham-like fist belonging to Liston, the malefic destroyer who is champion of the world."

--Arthur Daley, NY Post

"Clay should see a good psychiatrist."

--Rocky Marciano

Miami Beach Boxing Commission "10 Point Must Scoring System"	Miami Beach Boxing Commission "10 Point Must Scoring System"	Miami Beach Boxing Commission "10 Point Must Scoring System"	Miami Beach Boxing Commission "10 Point Must Scoring System"	Miami Beach Boxing Commission "10 Point Must Scoring System"	Miami Beach Boxing Commission "10 Point Must Scoring System"
EVENT: Mary	EVENT: Mary	EVENT: Mary	EVENT: Mary	EVENT: Mary	EVENT: Mary
ROUND 1	ROUND 1	ROUND 1	ROUND 1	ROUND 1	ROUND 1
MUST BE HANDED IN TO COMMISSION AT RINGSIDE AFTER END OF EACH ROUND.	MUST BE HANDED IN TO COMMISSION AT RINGSIDE AFTER END OF EACH ROUND.	MUST BE HANDED IN TO COMMISSION AT RINGSIDE AFTER END OF EACH ROUND.	MUST BE HANDED IN TO COMMISSION AT RINGSIDE AFTER END OF EACH ROUND.	MUST BE HANDED IN TO COMMISSION AT RINGSIDE AFTER END OF EACH ROUND.	MUST BE HANDED IN TO COMMISSION AT RINGSIDE AFTER END OF EACH ROUND.
WHITE CORNER / BLACK CORNER	WHITE CORNER / BLACK CORNER	WHITE CORNER / BLACK CORNER	WHITE CORNER / BLACK CORNER	WHITE CORNER / BLACK CORNER	WHITE CORNER / BLACK CORNER
NAME: Liston / NAME: Clay	NAME: Liston / NAME: Clay	NAME: Liston / NAME: Clay	NAME: Liston / NAME: Clay	NAME: Liston / NAME: Clay	NAME: Liston / NAME: Clay
9 POINTS / POINTS 10	9 POINTS / POINTS 10	9 POINTS / POINTS 10	9 POINTS / POINTS 10	9 POINTS / POINTS 10	9 POINTS / POINTS 10
Judge: JACOBSON	Judge: JACOBSON	Judge: JACOBSON	Judge: JACOBSON	Judge: JACOBSON	Judge: JACOBSON

The judges' score-cards for the first Clay-Liston fight.

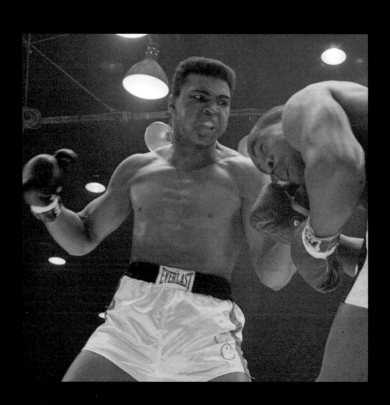

Stills from the first Clay-Liston fight, which Ali won in seven rounds, and the rematch a year later, when he knocked Liston out in the first.

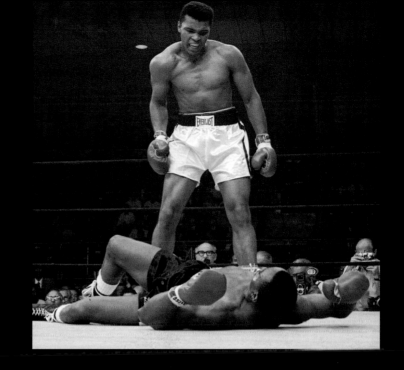

"It will go down in boxing history how the myth of Sonny Liston, The Great Inconquerable, was exploded in the flurry of hammering fists of a brash, brave, and talkative young man. Say all you will about Cassius and his great flow of language, his towering ego, his unorthodox manner of projecting himself. You must still admit that he puts the deeds behind the words and came through victoriously. "

—Jackie Robinson

מוסף שבועי

רשת המודיעין
של מס ההכנסה

■

הקרב
ליסטון-קליי

■

At Clay's victory press conference, the new champ, who'd become a close friend of Malcolm X, announced that he was a follower of Elijah Muhammad's Nation of Islam. And he was changing his name; Clay would now be known as Muhammad Ali. Above: A Hebrew language poster from the fight.

come out of that door, I'm going to break it down!"

You know that look of Liston's you hear so much about? Well, he sure had it on standing in that door that night. Man, he was tore up! He didn't know what to do. He wanted to come out there after me, but he was already in enough troubles with the police and everything. And you know, if a man figures you're crazy, he'll think twice before he acts, because he figures you're liable to do *anything*. But before he could make up his mind, the police came rushing in with all their sirens going, and they broke it up, telling us we would be arrested for disturbing the peace if we didn't get out of there. So we left. You can bet we laughed all the way to New York.

HALEY One doctor described your conduct at the weigh-in as "dangerously disturbed." Another said you acted "scared to death." And seasoned sportswriters used such terms as "hysterical" and "schizophrenic" in reporting your tantrum, for which you were fined twenty-five hundred dollars. What was the real story?

CLAY I would just say that it sounds like them doctors and sportswriters had been listening to each other. You know what they said and wrote them things for—to match in what they expected was about to happen. That's what I keep on telling you. If all of them had had their way, I wouldn't have been allowed in the ring.

> "Not many people know the quality of the mind he's got in there. He fools them. One forgets that though a clown never imitates a wise man, a wise man can imitate the clown. He is sensitive, very humble, yet shrewd—with as much untapped mental energy as he has physical power." —Malcolm X

HALEY Had you worked out a fight plan by this time?

CLAY I figured out my strategy and announced it *months* before the fight: "Float like a butterfly, sting like a bee," is what I said.

then on. It was my concentrating on that cut that let me get caught with the hardest punch I took, that long left. It rocked me back. But he either didn't realize how good I was hit or he was already getting tired, and he didn't press his chance. I sure heard the bell *that* time. I needed to get to my corner to get my head clear.

Starting in the third round, I saw his expression, how shook he was that we were still out there and *he* was the one cut and bleeding. He didn't know what to do. But I wasn't about to get careless, like Conn did that time against Joe Louis. This was supposed to be one of my coasting, resting rounds, but I couldn't waste no time. I needed one more good shot, for some more insurance with that eye. So when the bell rang, I just tested him, to see was he tiring, and he was; and then I got him into the ropes. It didn't take but one good combination. My left was square on his right eye, and a right under his left eye opened a deep gash. I knew it was deep, the way the blood spurted right out. I saw his face up close when he wiped his

glove at that cut and saw the blood. At that moment, let me tell you, he looked like he's going to look twenty years from now. Liston was tiring fast in the fourth, and I was coasting. We didn't neither one do very much. But you can bet it wasn't nobody in there complaining they wasn't getting their money's worth.

Then, in the fifth, all of a sudden, after one exchange of shots, there was a feeling in my eyes like some acid was in them. I could see just blurry. When the bell sounded, it felt like fire, and I could just make it back to my corner, telling Angelo, "I can't see!" And he was swabbing at my eyes. I could hear that excited announcer; he was having a fit. "Something seems to be wrong with Clay!" It sure was something wrong. I didn't care if it was a heavyweight title fight I had worked so long for, I wasn't going out there and get

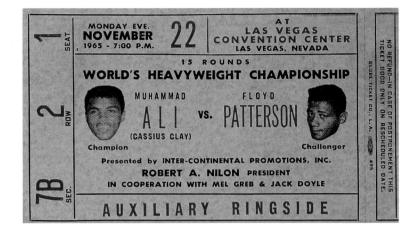

In 1965, Ali defended his crown against Floyd Patterson, whom Ali dubbed "The Rabbit" (" 'cause he's scared like a rabbit.") Before the fight, the champ showed up at Patterson's training camp with carrots and heads of lettuce.

"The bottom line is that Muhammad Ali always stood for what is right. He was born with that. He had a warrior's heart when he was born. He looked around to see how black people were treated, and he couldn't tolerate it. <u>He couldn't tolerate it.</u> And he is so special because he doesn't have a bitterness about him.... He has a love not just for black people, but for all good people—which does not get reported. Powerful people have a love for all people—that's how they have the strength to be warriors. The strongest warriors are those strong from the inside, not from their physical strength. You don't become a warrior because of your occupation. You become a warrior in your soul. Ali didn't let his occupation curtail his soul."

—Jim Brown

Ali-Patterson

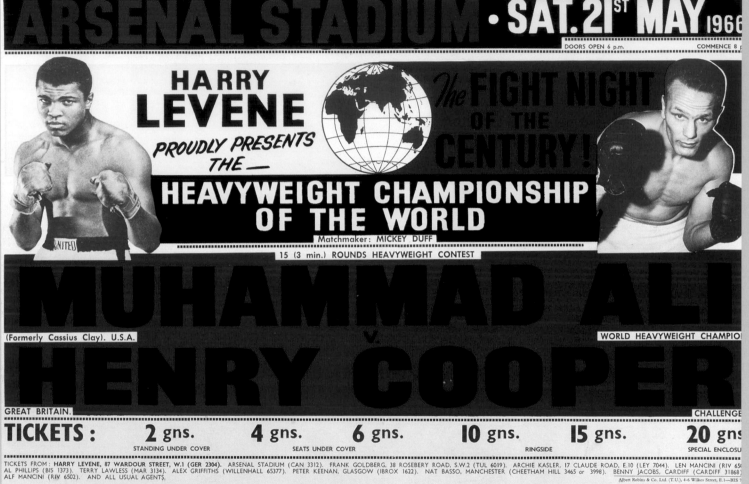

In 1966, Ali easily defended his crown in a rematch against Henry Cooper and then against Brian London. Cooper was a TKO, because of cuts on his face. "Blood scares me," admitted Ali after the fight. "I was more desperate than anyone when I saw him bleeding so badly."

EARLS COURT SATURDAY AUGUST 6TH 1966

DOORS OPEN 6.30   COMMENCE 8 p.m.

THE HEAVYWEIGHT CHAMPIONSHIP OF THE WORLD

THE FIGHT OF THE CENTURY   15 x 3 MIN. RDS.

PROUDLY PRESENTED BY **JACK SOLOMONS** AND **LAWRIE LEWIS**

MUHAMMAD ALI

(FORMERLY CASSIUS CLAY)

WORLD HEAVYWEIGHT CHAMPION

v

"BRITISH BULLDOG"

BRIAN LONDON

K.O'D ROGER RISCHER 1 RD. BEAT AMOS JOHNSON 7 RDS.

Both Rischer and Johnson have recently defeated Henry Cooper.

Amos Johnson (the only man to beat Clay) said at Liverpool that London may be too rough and strong for Clay

The unpredictable British Bulldog who loves a fight. Where Brian London performs you can always rely on excitement.

PRICES

| £4.4.0 | £6.6.0 | £10.10.0 | £15.15.0 | £21.0.0 |

GET YOUR TICKETS FROM:

Jack Solomons, 41 Gt. Windmill Street, W.1. Ger 9195/6
Thomas A'Beckett, 320 Old Kent Road, S.E.1. Rod 7334
G. Mancini, "Lord Palmerston," 648 King's Road, S.W.6. Rcn 4501

Alf Mancini, "Rifle," 80 Fulham Palace Road, W.6. Riv 6502
H. Gorman, 9 Lynton Place, Rumney, Cardiff 77023
Jim Smith, 102 Ophir Road, Northend, Portsmouth 63132
Lew Phillips, 177 Corporation Street, Birmingham. Cen 3552
Alex Griffiths, Deauville, Dingle Lane, Willenhall, Staffs.

Sam Docherty, 147 Renfield Street, Glasgow, C.2. Douglas 3662
Con Beynon, Stoneleigh Club, Porthcawl. 2696
Tony Viazzini, Station Cafe, Merthyr, 2695
Gus Demmy Promotions Ltd., 58a Swan Street, Manchester 4. Blackfriars 9248

Geo. Biddles, 169 Melton Road, Leicester. 62374
Lawrie Lewis, 92 West Drive, Cleveleys, Blackpool
Barney Eastwood, Barney Eastwood Promotions, 39 High Street, Belfast
Usual Agents and any Jack Solomons and Bud Flanagan Betting Shops

In 1967, Ernie Terrell refused to refer to the champ as "Ali." Instead, he called him Clay. This infuriated Ali: "I want to torture him. A clean knockout is too good for him." Sure enough, the champ didn't knock him out; he won in fifteen rounds and sent Terrell to the hospital for emergency surgery.

murdered because I couldn't see. Every time I blinked it hurt so bad I said, "Cut off my gloves, Angelo—leave me out of here." Then I heard the bell, and the referee, Barney Felix, yelled to me to get out there, and at the same time Angelo was pushing me up, shouting, "This is the big one, daddy. We aren't going to quit now!" And I was out there again, blinking. Angelo was shouting, "Stay away from him! Stay away!" I got my left in Liston's face and kept it there, kind of staving him off, and at the same time I knew where he was. I was praying he wouldn't guess what was the matter. But he had to see me blinking, and then he shook me with that left to the head and a lot of shots to the body. Now, I ain't too sorry it happened, because it proved I could take Liston's punching. He had found some respect for me, see? He wasn't going so much for the knockout; he was trying to hurt my body, then try for a kill. Man, in that round, my plans were *gone*. I was just trying to keep alive, hoping the tears would wash out my eyes. I could open them just enough to get a good glimpse of Liston, and then it hurt so bad I blinked them closed again. Liston was snorting like a horse. He was trying to hit me square, and I was just moving every which way, because I knew if he connected right, it could be all over right there.

But in the corner after that fifth round, the stuff pretty well washed out of my eyes. I could see again, and I was ready to carry the fight to Liston. And I was gaining my second wind now, as I had conditioned myself, to pace the fight, like I was telling you. My corner people knew it, and they were calling to me, "Get mad, baby!" They knew I was ready to go the next three rounds at top steam, and I knew I was going to make Liston look terrible. I hit him with eight punches in a row, until he doubled up. I remember thinking something like, "Yeah, you old sucker! You try to be so big and bad!" He was gone. He knew he couldn't last. It was the first time in the fight that I set myself flat-footed. I missed a right that might have dropped him. But I jabbed and jabbed at that cut under his eye, until it was wide open and bleeding worse than before. I knew he wasn't due to last much longer. Then, right at the end of the round, I rocked back his head with two left hooks.

I got back to my stool, and under me I could hear the press like they was gone wild. I twisted around and hollered down at the reporters right under me, "I'm gonna upset the world!" I never will forget how their faces was looking up at me like they couldn't believe it. I happened to be looking right at Liston when that warning buzzer sounded, and I didn't believe it when he spat out his mouthpiece. I just couldn't believe it—but there it was laying there. And then something just told me he wasn't coming out! I give a whoop and come off that stool like it was red hot. It's a funny thing, but I wasn't even thinking about Liston—I was thinking about nothing but that hypocrite press. All of them down there had wrote so much about me bound to get killed by the big fists. It was even rumors that right after the weigh-in I had been taken to the asylum somewhere, and another rumor that I had caught a plane and run off. I couldn't think about nothing but all that. I went dancing around the ring, hollering down at them reporters, "Eat your words! Eat! Eat!" And I hollered at the people, "I am the *king*!"

HALEY What or who made you decide to join the Muslims? **CLAY** Nobody or nothing *made* me decide. I make up my mind for myself. In 1960 in Miami I was training for a fight. It wasn't long after I had won the 1960 Olympic Gold Medal over there in Rome. Herb Siler was the fellow I was going to fight, I remember. I put him on the floor in four. Anyway, one day this Muslim minister came to meet me and he asked me wouldn't I like to come to his mosque and hear about the history of my forefathers. I never had heard no black man talking about no forefathers, except that they were slaves, so I went to a meeting. And this minister started teaching, and the things he said really shook me up. Things like that we twenty million black people in America didn't know our true identities, or even our true family names. And we were the direct descendants of black men and women stolen from a rich black

"Ali in front of a camera is something to behold. He is a natural performer, a natural talent. . . . Most fighters play it pretty close to the vest, but Ali isn't afraid to show a little bit of himself. His ability to put himself in front of people led people to love him. And what has surprised me over the years is that even past his public image, he is completely without animus. He doesn't have a case against anyone. Despite his religion and the stance he took on the draft, despite the disagreements he had, it was never personal. It was never 'me against them.' He was always available to all of us. A man who can take a stand and still do that is a remarkable man. I adore him and the way he adores people. . . ."

—James Earl Jones

"I am the greatest! I shook up the world! I don't have a mark on my face! I'm pretty! I'm a bad man! You must listen to me! I can't be beat!.... I'm the pretti-est thing that ever lived!"

—Muhammad Ali

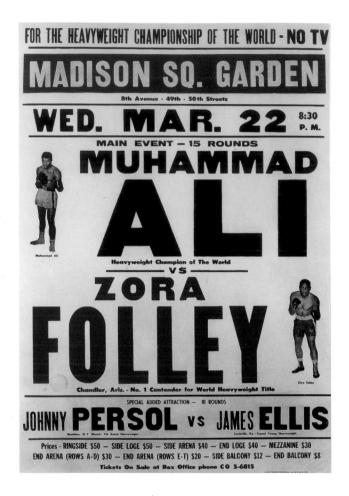

FOR THE HEAVYWEIGHT CHAMPIONSHIP OF THE WORLD · NO TV

MADISON SQ. GARDEN

8th Avenue · 49th · 50th Streets

WED. MAR. 22 8:30 P.M.

MAIN EVENT — 15 ROUNDS

MUHAMMAD

ALI

Heavyweight Champion of The World

VS

ZORA

FOLLEY

Chandler, Ariz. - No. 1 Contender for World Heavyweight Title

SPECIAL ADDED ATTRACTION — 10 ROUNDS

JOHNNY PERSOL VS JAMES ELLIS

Brooklyn, N.Y. World's 7th Rated Heavyweight   Louisville, Ky.- Feared Young Heavyweight

Prices - RINGSIDE $50 — SIDE LOGE $50 — SIDE ARENA $40 — END LOGE $40 — MEZZANINE $30
END ARENA (ROWS A-D) $30 — END ARENA (ROWS E-T) $20 — SIDE BALCONY $12 — END BALCONY $8

Tickets On Sale at Box Office phone CO 5-6815

Following his victory in the Zora Folley fight, Ali was forced into retirement for refusing to enlist for military service in the Vietnam War. As he put it: "I ain't got no quarrel with them Vietcong." During a three-year hiatus, he earned a living by making motivational speeches.

continent and brought here and stripped of all knowledge of themselves and taught to hate themselves and their kind. And that's how us so-called "Negroes" had come to be the only race among mankind that loved its enemies. Now, I'm the kind that catches on quick. I said to myself, listen here, this man's *saying* something! I hope don't nobody never hit me in the ring hard as it did when that brother minister said the Chinese are named after China, Russians after Russia, Cubans after Cuba, Italians after Italy, the English after England, and clear on down the line everybody was named for somewhere he could call home, except us. He said, "What country are we so-called 'Negroes' named for? *No* country! We are just a lost race." Well, *boom*! That really shook me up.

HALEY How has it changed your life?
CLAY In every way. It's pulled me up and cleaned me up as a human being.

HALEY Can you be more explicit?
CLAY Well, before I became a Muslim, I used to drink. Yes, I did. The truth is the truth. And after I had fought and beat somebody, I didn't hardly go nowhere without two big, pretty women beside me. But my change is one of the things that will mark me as a great man in history. When you can live righteous in the hell of North America—when a man can control his life, his physical needs, his lower self, he elevates himself. The downfall of so many great men is that they haven't been able to control their appetite for women.

HALEY But you have?
CLAY We Muslims don't touch a woman unless we're married to her.

HALEY Are you saying that you don't have affairs with women?

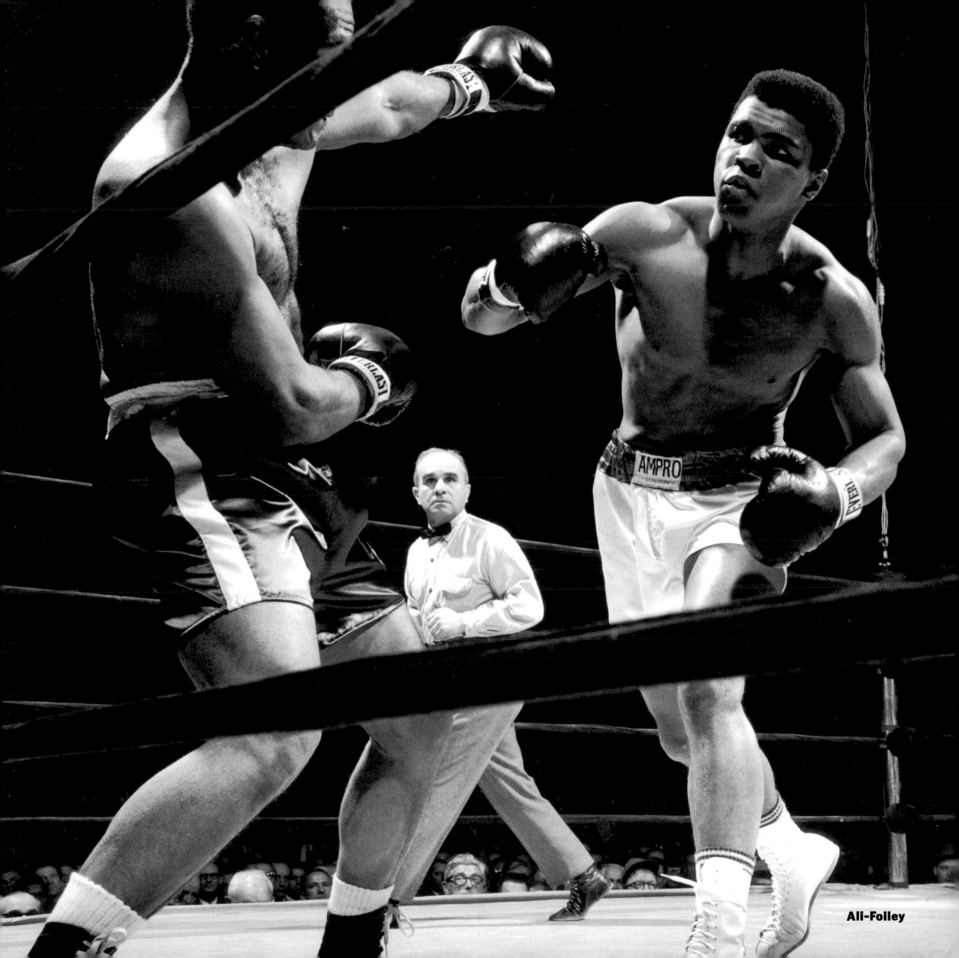

Ali-Folley

"I never thought of myself as great when I refused to go in the Army. All I did was stand up for what I believed. There were people who thought the war in Vietnam was right. And those people, if they went to war, acted just as brave as I did.... Freedom means being able to follow your religion, but it also means carrying the responsibility to choose between right and wrong. So when the time came for me to make up my mind about going in the Army, I knew people were dying in Vietnam for nothing and I should live by what I thought was right. I wanted America to be America. And now the whole world knows that."

—Muhammad Ali

CLAY I don't even kiss a woman. I'm ashamed of myself, but sometimes I've caught myself wishing I had found Islam about five years from now, maybe—with all the temptations I have to resist. But I don't even kiss none, because you get too close, it's almost impossible to stop. I'm a young man, you know, in the prime of life.

HALEY Are there any active heavyweights whom you rate as title contenders?
CLAY Not in my class, of course....

HALEY Just you?
CLAY Just me.

HALEY Are you the greatest now fighting, or the greatest in boxing history?
CLAY Now, a whole lot of people ain't going to like this. But I'm going to tell you the truth—you asked me. It's too many great old champions to go listing them one by one. But ain't no need to. I think that Joe Louis, in his prime, could have whipped them all—I mean anyone you want to name. And I would have beat Louis. Now, look—people don't like to face the facts. All they can think about is Joe Louis' punch. Well, he did have a deadly punch, just like Liston has a deadly punch. But if Louis didn't hit nothing but air, like Liston didn't with me, then we got to look at other things. Even if Louis did hit me a few times, remember they all said Liston was a tougher one-punch man than even Joe Louis. And I took some of Liston's best shots. Remember that. Then, too, I'm taller than Louis. But I tell you what would decide the fight: I'm *faster* than Louis was. No, Louis and none of the rest of them couldn't whip me. Look—it ain't *never* been another fighter like me. Ain't never been no *nothing* like me.

Ali with reporter Howard Cosell, one of his staunchest allies during the suspension of his boxing license.

"I loved Ali; I still do. As a young black, at times I was ashamed of my color; I was ashamed of my hair. And Ali made me proud. I'm just as happy being black now as you are being white, and Ali was a part of that growing process."

1970s by Norman Mailer

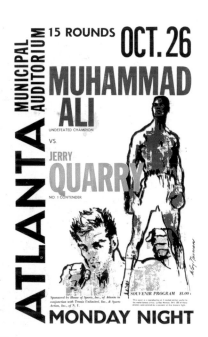

Fight posters from Ali's first fight with Jerry Quarry. He defeated Quarry twice by TKO. "Ain't this an easy way to make a livin'?" Ali yelled to the crowd after the second fight.

Rumble in the Jungle
Defending the Crown

There is always a shock

in seeing him again. Not *live* as in television but standing before you, looking his best. Then the World's Greatest Athlete is in danger of being our most beautiful man, and the vocabulary of Camp is doomed to appear. Women draw an *audible* breath. Men look *down*. They are reminded again of their lack of worth. If Ali never opened his mouth to quiver the jellies of public opinion, he would still inspire love and hate. For he is the Prince of Heaven—so says the silence around his body when he is luminous....

Solemnly, Bundini handed Ali the white African robe which the fighter had selected. Then everybody in the dressing room was on their way, a long file of twenty men who pushed and were hustled through a platoon of soldiers standing outside the door and then in a gang's rush in a full company of other soldiers were racing through the gray cement-brick corridors with their long-gone echoes of rifle shots and death. They emerged into open air, into the surrealistic bliss and green air of stadium grass under electric lights, and a cheer of no vast volume went up at the sight of Ali, but then the crowd had been waiting through an empty hour with

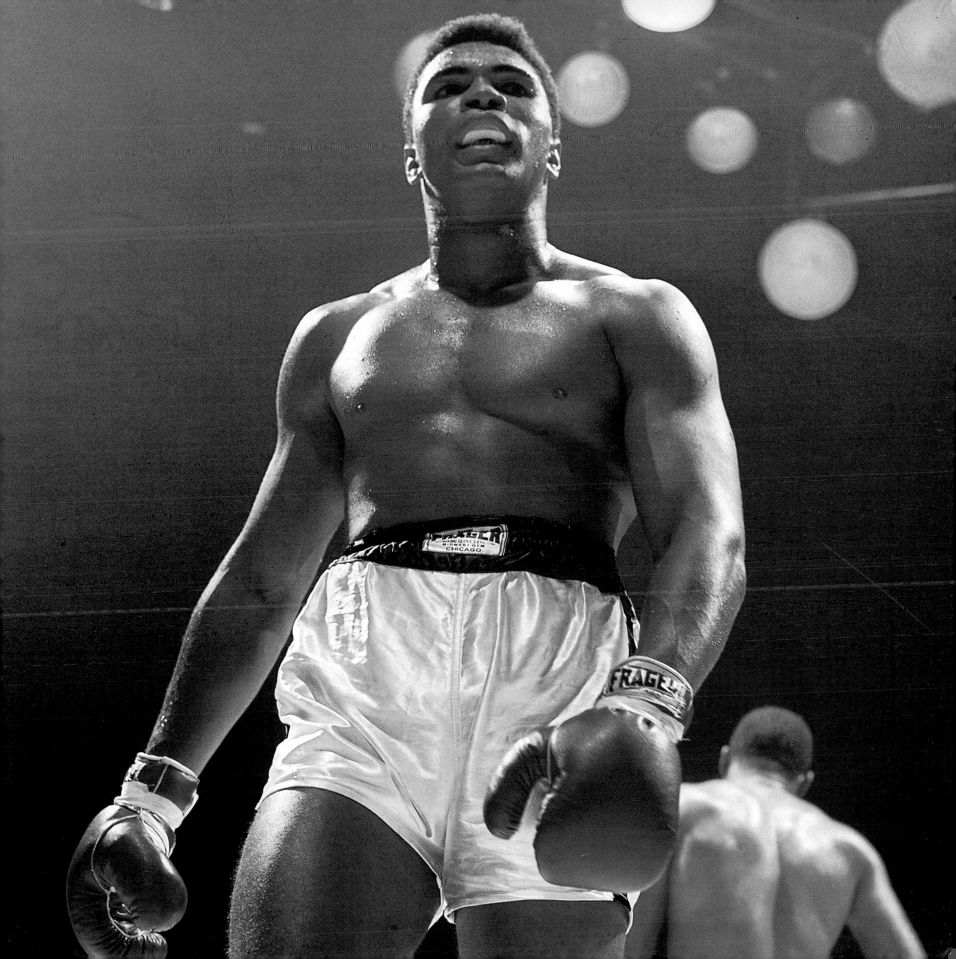

Bonavena was Ali's second fight after returning from exile. The awkward Argentinian whom Ali nicknamed "The Beast," had gone twenty-five rounds with Joe Frazier and had never been knocked out. And though not regarded as one of his better fights, Ali dropped Bonavena three times in the fifteenth round. Screamed Ali after the fight: "I want Joe Frazier!"

DIRECT FROM RINGSIDE · MADISON SQ. GARDEN, N.Y.C.
See it "LIVE" On BIG Screen Closed Circuit TV
AT
MIAMI BEACH
CONVENTION HALL
17th St. and Washington Ave.
AIR CONDITIONED
UNDER DIRECTION OF CHRIS DUNDEE
AUSPICES VFW POST 3559
PHONE 538-4304 or 531-0477 FOR RESERVATIONS
Admission $5.00
DOORS OPEN 8:00 PM
Reserved $7.00 & $10

DEC. 7 MON EVE
15 ROUNDS

Undefeated CASSIUS MUHAMAD ALI CLAY VS Challenger Oscar "Ringo" BONAVENA

NO HOME TV

PLUS EXTRA 10 ROUND SPECIAL ATTRACTION
DONATO PADUANO VS KEN BUCHANAN
CANADIAN WELTERWEIGHT CHAMPION
WORLD LIGHTWEIGHT CHAMPION
TICKETS ON SALE AT MIAMI BEACH AUDITORIUM & ALL SEARS STORES

Sept. 30, 1975
"A thrilla in Manila"

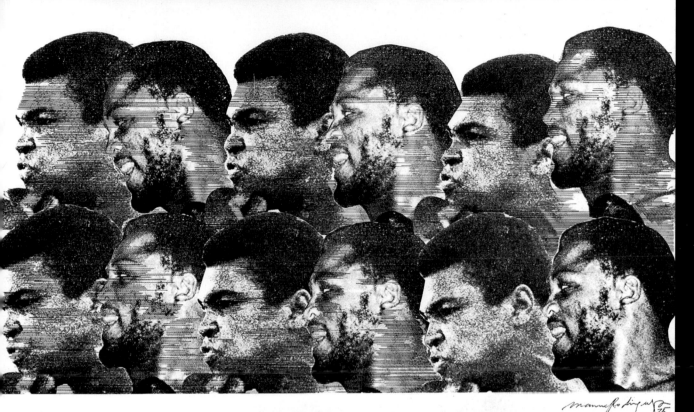

ALI-FRAZIER
FIGHT OF A LIFETIME
PHILIPPINES

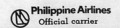
Official carrier

"I don't think two big men ever fought fights like me and Joe Frazier. One fight, maybe. But three times; we were the only ones. Of all the men I fought in boxing, Sonny Liston was the scariest; George Foreman was the most powerful; Floyd Patterson was the most skilled as a boxer. But the roughest and toughest was Joe Frazier. He brought out the best in me, and the best fight we fought was in Manila. That fight, I could feel something happening to me. Something different from what I'd felt in fights before. And God blessed me that day. He's blessed me many times, and that fight in Manila was one of them. It was like I took myself as far as I could go, and then God took me the rest of the way. So I'm sorry Joe Frazier is mad at me. I'm sorry I hurt him. Joe Frazier is a good man. I couldn't have done what I did without him, and he couldn't have done what he did without me. And if God ever calls me to a holy war, I want Joe Frazier fighting beside me."
—Muhammad Ali

"The Thrilla in Manila was the best fight I've ever seen. As it unfolded, everybody at ringside understood they were watching greatness. From the third round on, it just kept building. The ebb and flow was incredible. In the sixth round, Frazier hit Ali with a left hook that's the hardest punch I've ever seen.... Ali's head turned like it was on a swivel, and his response was to look at Frazier and say, 'They told me Joe Frazier was washed up.' And Frazier answered, 'They lied.' The pace never eased; it was hell the whole way. I've never seen two people give more, ever. And I've never seen a film of that fight. I don't have to. I remember it like it was yesterday."

The early part of the decade saw Ali fight a rapid succession of less than stellar boxers. Jimmy Ellis, a childhood friend of Ali's, was stopped easily in the twelfth round. Then it was Buster Mathis; after the fight he was reported to have approached Ali in tears, thanking him for the opportunity to make money. Said Ali of the opinion he had been soft on Mathis: "How am I goin' to sleep if I just killed a man in front of his wife and son just to satisfy you writers?" Six weeks later Ali traveled to Switzerland to fight the German ex-butcher, Jurgin Blin, knocking him out in the seventh round. Unimpressive victories over Mac Foster and George Chuvalo preceded a second knockout of Jerry Quarry. Four weeks later it was

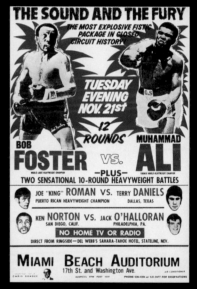

off to Dublin for a match with Al "Blue" Lewis, then a third victory over Patterson, followed by a pummeling of Bob Foster, and a relatively monotonous twelve-round decision over England's Joe Bugner. Meanwhile, Joe Frazier had lost the belt to hard-hitting George Foreman, setting up a showdown between Ali and Foreman. But first Ali had to get through eighth-ranked Ken Norton.

They circled again. They feinted. They started in on one another and drew back. It was as if each held a gun. If one fired and missed, the other was certain to hit....

Ali was not dancing. Rather he was bouncing from side to side looking for an opportunity to attack. So was Foreman. Maybe fifteen seconds went by. Suddenly Ali hit him again. It was again a right hand. Again it was hard. The sound of a bat thunking into a watermelon was heard around the ring. Once more Foreman charged after the blow, and once more Ali took him around the neck with his right arm, then stuck his left glove in Foreman's right armpit. Foreman could not start to swing. It was a nimble part of the advanced course for tying up a fighter. The referee broke the clinch. Again they moved through invisible reaches of attraction and repulsion, darting forward, sliding to the side, cocking their heads, each trying to strike an itch to panic in the other, two big men fast as pumas, charged as tigers—unseen sparks came off their moves. Ali hit him again, straight left, then a straight right. Foreman responded like a bull. He roared forward. A dangerous bull His gloves were out like horns. No room for Ali to dance to the side, stick him and move, hit him and move. Ali went back, feinted, went back again, was on the ropes. Foreman had cut him off. The fight was thirty seconds old, and Foreman had driven him to the ropes. Ali had not even tried to get around those outstretched gloves so ready to cuff him, rough him, break his grace, no, retreating, Ali collected his toll. He hit Foreman with another left and another right.

Still a wail went up from the crowd. They saw Ali on the ropes. Who had talked of anything but how long Ali could keep away? Now he was trapped, so soon. Yet Foreman was

> "In the 1970s, when Ali was trotting the globe, there were whole countries that couldn't pick Jimmy Carter out of a lineup but recognized Ali at a glance. His face was the most familiar on earth, and wherever he went the whispers always went up—"Ali . . . Ali . . . .""
>
> —William Nack

Journeyman boxer Chuvalo's claim to fame was that he had never been knocked down. One observer called his fighting style "left chin to the right hand." Ali's nickname for Chuvalo was "The Washerwoman" because of his arms-flailing style. Ali pummeled Chuvalo for fifteen rounds, yet Chuvalo never went down.

"He might have been the best heavy-weight who ever lived, a man with an astonishing range of skills, with fast hands and beautiful legs, a fighter who made a brutal sport contain the illusion of beauty. His fights resembled some bloody offshoot of ballet, choreographed in some dark region of his mind, a place where violence and control and courage met to forge a champion. Ten times he climbed through those red velvet ropes to fight for the heavyweight champi-onship of the world. Ten times he won, and each time he was better."

"He . . . has a sense of himself so firmly entrenched that it seems to hover, at times, in that nervous limbo between egomania and genuine invulnerability. He honestly believes he can handle it all; and he has almost two decades of evidence to back him up . . . ."

—Hunter S. Thompson

61

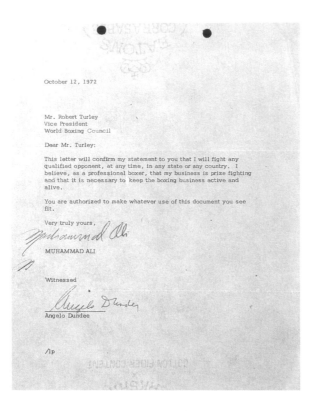

This October 12, 1972 letter written by Ali to Robert Turley, vice president of the World Boxing Council, states that "I will fight any qualified opponent, at any time, in any state or any country. I believe, as a professional boxer, that my business is prize fighting and that it is necessary to keep the boxing business active and alive. You are authorized to make whatever use of this document you see fit."

off his aim. Ali's last left and right had checked him. Foreman's punches were not ready and Ali parried, Ali blocked. They clinched. The referee broke it. Ali was off the ropes with ease.

To celebrate, he hit Foreman another straight right. Up and down the press rows, one exclamation was leaping, "He's hitting him with *rights*." Ali had not punched with such authority in seven years. Champions do not hit other champions with right-hand leads. Not in the first round. It is the most difficult and dangerous punch....

With everybody screaming, Ali now hit Foreman with a right. Foreman hit him back with a left and a right. Now they each landed blows. Everybody was shaking their head at the bell. What a round!....

David Frost, Jim Brown, and Joe Frazier [are] talking between rounds.... Jim Brown may have said last night that Ali had no chance, but Brown is one athlete who will report what he sees. "Great round for Muhammad Ali," he comments. "He did a fantastic job, although I don't think he can keep up this pace."

Sullenly, Joe Frazier disagrees. "Round was even . . . very close."

David Frost: "You wouldn't call that round for Ali?"

Joe is not there to root Ali home, not after Ali called him ignorant.

> "Ali was a showman. He brought the eyes of the world toward boxing. But he could back up what he said."
> —Jim Brown

Foreman sits on his stool listening to Sadler. His face is bemused as if he has learned more than he is accustomed to in the last few minutes and the sensation is half agreeable. He has certainly learned that Ali can hit. Already his face shows bumps and welts. Ali is also a better wrestler than any fighter he has faced. Better able to agitate him. He sits back to rest the sore heat of his lungs after the boil of his fury in the last round. He brings himself to smile at someone at ringside. The smile is forced. Across the ring, Ali spits into the bowl held out for him and looks wide awake. His eyes are as alive as a ghetto adolescent walking down a strange turf. Just before the bell, he stands up in his corner and leads a cheer. Ali's arm pumps the air to inspire the crowd, and he makes a point of glowering at Foreman. Abruptly, right after the bell, his mood takes a change.

As Foreman comes out Ali goes back to the ropes, no, lets himself be driven to the corner, the worst place a fighter can be, worst place by all established comprehension of boxing. In the corner you cannot slip to the side, cannot go backward. You must fight your way out. With the screech that comes up from a crowd when one car tries to pass another in a race, Foreman was in to move on Ali, and Ali fought the good rat fight of the corner, his gloves thrown with frantic speed at Foreman's gloves....

But then Ali must have come to a first assessment of assets and weaknesses, for—somewhere in the unremarked middle of the round—he must have made a decision on how to shape the rest of the fight. He did not seem able to hurt Foreman critically with those right-hand leads. Nor was he stronger than Foreman except when wrestling on his neck, and certainly he could not afford any more of those episodes where he held onto Foreman even as George was hitting him. It was costly in points, painful, and won nothing. On the other hand, it was too soon to dance. Too rapid would be the drain on his stamina. So the time had come to see if he could outbox Foreman while lying on the ropes. It had been his option from the beginning and it was the most dangerous option he had. For so long as Foreman had strength, the ropes would prove about as safe as riding a unicycle on a parapet. Ali introduced his grand theme. He lay back on the ropes in the middle of the second round, and from that position he would work for the rest of the fight, reclining at an angle of ten and twenty degrees from the vertical and sometimes even further, a cramped near-tortured angle from which to box.

Of course Ali had been preparing for just this hour over the last ten years. For ten years he had been practicing to fight

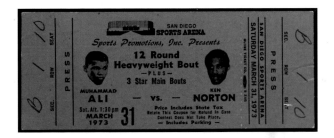

Ken Norton was a virtual unknown before his match with Ali in March, 1973, having earned a total of $300 in his previous fight. But Norton's straight-ahead boxing style, and one "lucky" punch that broke Ali's jaw, quickly introduced a new force in the boxing circuit. Said Ali of Norton: "I took a nobody and created a monster."

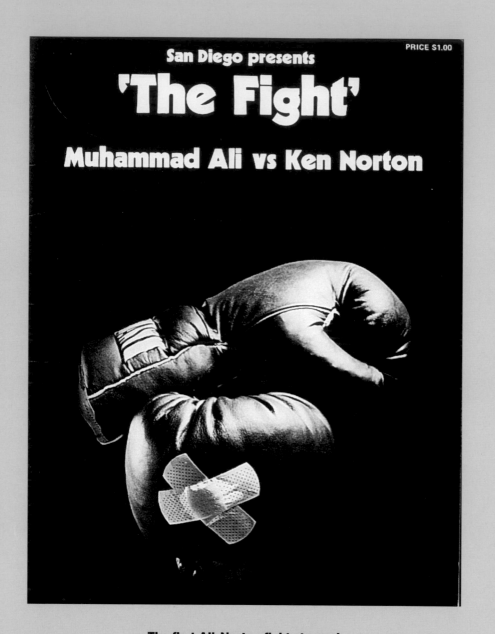

San Diego presents

'The Fight'

Muhammad Ali vs Ken Norton

The first Ali-Norton fight stunned everyone, perhaps Ali most of all. Norton connected in the second round with a right hand that broke Ali's jaw. They fought ten more rounds before Norton was awarded the victory by decision.

"You think the world was shocked when
   Nixon resigned

Wait till I whup George Foreman's behind.

Float like a butterfly, sting like a bee
His hands can't hit what his eyes can't see.
Now you see me, now you don't
George thinks he will, but I know he won't.

I done wrassled with an alligator
I done tussled with a whale
Only last week I murdered a rock
Injured a stone, hospitalized a brick.
I'm so mean I make medicine sick."

—Muhammad Ali

powerful sluggers who beat on your belly while you lay on the ropes. So he took up his station with confidence, shoulders parallel to the edge of the ring. In this posture his right would have no more impact than a straight left but he could find himself in position to cover his head with both gloves, and his belly with his elbows, he could rock and sway, lean so far back Foreman must fall on him. Should Foreman pause from the fatigue of throwing punches, Ali could bounce off the ropes and sting him, jolt him, make him look clumsy, mock him, rouse his anger, which might yet wear Foreman out more than anything else. In this position, Ali could even hurt him. A jab hurts if you run into it, and Foreman is always coming in. Still, Ali is in the position of a man bowing and ducking in a doorway while another man comes at him with two clubs. Foreman comes on with his two clubs. In the first exchange he hits Ali about six times while Ali is returning only one blow. Yet the punches to Ali's head seem not to bother him; he is swallowing the impact with his entire body. He is like a spring on the ropes. Blows seem to pass through him as if he

"There was a time in my life when I was sort of unfriendly and Zaire was part of that period. I was going to knock Ali's block off, and the thought of doing it didn't bother me at all." —George Foreman

is congested in his joints. Encouraged by the recognition that he can live with these blows, he begins to taunt Foreman. "Can you hit?" he calls out. "You can't hit. You push!" Since his head has been in range of Foreman's gloves, Foreman lunges at him. Back goes Ali's head like the carnival boy ducking baseballs. Wham to you, goes Ali, catapulting back. Bing and sting! Now Foreman is missing and Ali is hitting....

It seems like eight rounds have passed yet we've only finished two.

Everybody has wondered whether Ali can get through the first few rounds and take Foreman's punch. Now the problem has been refined: Can he dismantle Foreman's strength before he uses up his own wit?

To Carol + Russ

From
Muhammad
Ali
Peace
1977

Ali-Foreman

OFFICIAL PRESS POLL
ALI - FOREMAN

NAME	PAPER	Selection
Muhammad Ali		
Samuel Clark	Black Audio Network	Ali – 12th round
MEHMET BIBER	HURRMET. ALIBAS BIBER	ALI
TEO BETTI	IL MESSAGGERO (ITALY)	FOREMAN 10 down
Tom Callahan	Cincinnati Enquirer	FOREMAN 1st Round
WILL GRIMSLEY	ASSOCIATED PRESS-NY	ALI 15 ROUNDS
BILL CARDOSO	NEW TIMES	ALI TKO 12 ~~8~~
Van den Berg Jan	BRT - Laatste N.	~~Ali 12~~
COLIN HART	THE SUN - LONDON	ALI - 11
BOB OTTUM	SPORTS ILLUSTRATED NEW YORK	FOREMAN
Gede Kelly	ALI's Camp	Ali's
Jim BARNIAK	Philadelphia Bulletin	Foreman 4
Sonia KATCHIAN	CAMMA - Sports Illustrated	Ali - 9th round
BUDD SCHULBERG	NEWSDAY	ALI TKO 13 FOREMAN WON'T CAN OUT FOR
Tom Cushman	Phil. Daily News	Foreman TKO 6
NORM MAILER	PLAYBOY	ALI 14th
BOURDIER	AP - Miami	Foreman - 2
Bill CAPLAN	Promotion	FOREMAN - 3
DAVE ANDERSON	NY TIMES	FOREMAN 1
Ben Wott	German TV	Ali in 11
EARL LAW	WVON Radio - Chicago	ALI 10

A listing of writers and personalities connected to the Ali-Foreman fight and their predictions of the outcome. Despite Foreman being a huge favorite, the lists have Ali with a 24-20 edge.

All the while Ali was talking. "Come on, George, show me something," he would say. "Can't you fight harder? That ain't hard. I thought you was the Champion, I thought you had punches," and Foreman working like a bricklayer running up a pyramid to set his bricks would snort and lance his arms in sudden unexpected directions and try to catch Ali bouncing on the rope, Ali who was becoming more confirmed every minute in the sinecure of the rope, but at the end of the round, Foreman caught him with the best punch he had thrown in many a minute, landing just before the bell, and as he turned to leave Ali, he said clearly, "How's that?"

Like much of the greatness, the beginnings were unremarked. Foreman ended the fourth round well, but expectation was circling ringside that a monumental upset could be shaping. Even Joe Frazier was admitting that George was "not being calm." It took John Daly to blurt out cheerfully to David Frost, "Ali is winning all the way for me and I think he's going to take it within another four rounds!"

Foreman didn't think so. There had been that sniff of victory in the fourth, the good punch which landed—"How's that?" He came out in the fifth with the conviction that if force had not prevailed against Ali up to now, more force was the answer, considerably more force than Ali had ever seen. If Foreman's face was battered to lumps and his legs were moving like wheels with a piece chipped out of the rim, if his arms were beginning to sear in the lava of exhaustion and his breath came roaring to his lungs like the blast from a bed of fire, still he was a prodigy of strength, he was the prodigy, he could live through states of torture and hurl his cannonade when others could not lift their arms, he had been trained for endurance even more than execution and back in Pendleton when first working for this fight had once boxed fifteen rounds with half a dozen sparring partners coming on in two-round shifts while Foreman was permitted only thirty

> "During rope a dope, I laid on the ropes and said: 'Punch, sucker. That's a sissy punch. Now it's my turn.'"
>
> — Muhammad Ali

seconds of rest between each round. He could go, he could go and go, he was tireless in the arms, yes, could knock down a forest, take it down all by himself, and he set out now to chop Ali down....

So began the third act of the fight. Not often was there a better end to a second act than Foreman's failure to destroy Ali on the ropes. But the last scenes would present another problem. How was the final curtain to be found? For if Foreman was exhausted, Ali was weary. He had hit Foreman harder than he had ever hit anyone. He had hit him often. Foreman's head must by now be equal to a piece of vulcanized rubber. Conceivably you could beat on him all night and nothing more would happen. There is a threshold to the knockout. When it comes close but is not crossed, then a man can stagger around the ring forever. He has received his terrible message and he is still standing.... So Ali was obliged to produce still one more surprise. If not, the unhappiest threat would present itself as he and Foreman stumbled through the remaining rounds....

Ali needed rest. The next two minutes turned into the slowest two minutes of the fight. Foreman kept pushing Ali to the ropes out of habit, a dogged forward motion that enabled George to rest in his fashion, the only way he still knew, which was to lean on the opponent. Ali was by now so delighted with the advantages of the ropes that he fell back on them like a man returning home in quiet triumph, yes, settled in with the weary pleasure of a working man getting back into bed after a long day to be treated to a little of God's joy by his hardworking wife. He was almost tender with Foreman's laboring advance, holding him softly and kindly by the neck. Then he stung him with right and left karate shots from the shoulder. Foreman was now so arm-weary he could begin a punch only by lurching forward until his momentum encouraged a movement of the arm. He looked like a drunk, or rather a somnambulist, in a dance marathon. It would be wise to get him through the kill without ever waking him up. While it ought to be a simple matter to knock him down, there might not be enough violence left in the spirit of this ring to knock

"George was the most powerful puncher of his time. And what I remember most about that fight was, Ali rushed out at the opening bell, showing no fear, and struck George on top of the head. Right at the start, George knew he had something different to contend with. But George only knew one way to fight, so he swung and he swung, and he pinned Ali up against the ropes, determined to wear

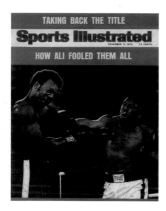

him down. At first, that seemed like a fine strategy. Everything we'd planned was designed to get Ali on the ropes, where George could hit him. But once George got him there, and when Ali stayed there, George didn't know what to do.... And when George's punches did land, Ali took them with a marvelous show of disdain and managed to convince George that George couldn't punch. Ali had him thinking and worrying, and when George got tired against a skilled warrior like Ali, that was the beginning of the end. In fact, that was the end."

—Archie Moore

him out. So the shock of finding himself on the floor could prove a stimulant. His ego might reappear: once on the floor, he was a champion in dramatic danger of losing his title—that is an unmeasurable source of energy. Ali was now taking in the reactions of Foreman's head the way a bullfighter lines up a bull before going in over the horns for the kill....

Jim Brown was saying, "This man, Muhammad Ali, is unreal." When Jim used the word, it was a compliment. Whatever was real, Jim Brown could dominate. And Frazier added his humor, "I would say right now my man is not in the lead. I got a feeling George is not going to make it...."

Foreman's legs were now hitched into an ungainly prance like a horse high-stepping along a road full of rocks. Stung for the hundredth time with a cruel blow, his response was to hurl back a left hook that proved so wild he almost catapulted through the ropes. Then for an instant, his back and neck were open to Ali, who cocked a punch but did not throw it, as though to demonstrate for an instant to the world that he did not want to flaw this fight with any blow reminiscent of the thuds Foreman had sent to the back of the head of Norton and Roman and Frazier. So Ali posed with that punch, then moved away. Now for the second time in the fight he had found Foreman between himself and the ropes and had done nothing.

Well, George came off the ropes and pursued Ali like a man chasing a cat. The wild punch seemed to have refreshed him by its promise that some of his power was back. If his biggest punches were missing, at least they were big. Once again he might be his own prodigy of strength. Now there were flurries on the ropes which had an echo of the great bombardment in the fifth round. And still Ali taunted him, still the dialogue went on. "Fight hard," said Ali, "I thought you had some punches. You're a weak man. You're all used up." After a while, Foreman's punches were whistling less than his breath. For the eighteenth time Ali's corner was screaming, "Get off the ropes. Knock him out. Take him home!" Foreman had used up the store of force he transported from the seventh to the eighth. He pawed at Ali like an infant six

"Muhammad amazed me; I'll admit it. He out-thought me; he out-fought me. That night, he was just the better man in the ring. Before the fight, I thought I'd knock him out easy. One round, two rounds. I was very confident. And what I remember most about the fight was, I went out and hit Muhammad with the hardest shot to the body I ever delivered to any opponent. Anybody else in the world would have crumbled. Muhammad cringed; I could see it hurt. And then he looked at me; he had that look in his eyes, that's the main thing I remember about the fight.... After the fight, for a while I was bitter. I had all sorts of excuses.... I should have just said the best man won, but I'd never lost before so I didn't know how to lose. I fought that fight over in my head a thousand times. And then, finally, I realized I'd lost to a great champion; probably the greatest of all time. He won fair and square, and now I'm just proud to be part of the Ali legend. If people mention my name with his from time to time, that's enough for me. That, and I hope Muhammad likes me, because I like him. I like him a lot."

—George Foreman

Give *The White Guy A Break*"
ALI·WEPNER WORLD HEAVY WEIGHT CHAMPIONSHIP FIGHT

After the Rumble in the Jungle, Ali defended his heavyweight crown ten times over a span of two-and-a-half years. Ali's first title defense came against unranked liquor salesman Chuck "The Bayonne Bleeder" Wepner. One columnist called it "More transfusion than boxing match." The fight is probably most notable for being Sylvester Stallone's inspiration for the "Rocky" films.

feet tall waving its uncoordinated battle arm.

With twenty seconds left to the round, Ali attacked. By his own measure, by that measure of twenty years of boxing, with the knowledge of all he had learned of what could and could not be done at any instant in the ring, he chose this as the occasion and lying on the ropes, he hit Foreman with a right and left, then came off the ropes to hit him with a left and a right. Into this last right hand he put his glove and his forearm again, a head-stupefying punch that sent Foreman reeling forward. As he went by, Ali hit him on the side of the jaw with a right, and darted away from the ropes in such a way as to put Foreman next to them. For the first time in the entire fight he had cut off the ring on Foreman. Now Ali struck him a combination of punches fast as the punches of the first round, but harder and more consecutive, three capital rights in a row struck Foreman, then a left, and for an instant on Foreman's face appeared the knowledge that he was in danger and must start to look to his last protection. His opponent was attacking, and there were no ropes behind the opponent. What a dislocation: the axes of his existence were reversed! He was the man on the ropes! Then a big projectile exactly the size of a fist in a glove drove into the middle of Foreman's mind, the best punch of the startled night, the blow Ali saved for a career. Foreman's arms flew out to the side like a man with a parachute jumping out of a plane, and in this doubled-over position he tried to wander out to the center of the ring. All the while his eyes were on Ali and he looked up with no anger as if Ali, indeed, was the man he knew best in the world and would see him on his dying day. Vertigo took George Foreman and revolved him. Still bowing from the waist in this uncomprehending position, eyes on Muhammad Ali all the way, he started to tumble and topple and fall even as he did not wish to go down. His mind was held with magnets high as his championship and his body was seeking the ground. He went over like a six-foot sixty-year-old butler who has just heard tragic news, yes, fell over all of a long collapsing two seconds, down came the Champion in sections and Ali revolved with him in a close

Despite being urged to retire by many in his camp, at thirty-five, Ali stepped into the ring against Earnie Shavers. In the second round Shavers landed a punch Ali said was "next to Joe Frazier the hardest I ever got hit." But Ali survived to win his fifty-fifth fight with a last minute barrage that left Shavers out on his feet. "I'm tired," Ali moaned after the fight. "I'm so damned tired."

Not all of Ali's fights held the importance or drama of the heavyweight championship. In fact, many could hardly be called fights at all. In the match with Japanese wrestler Antonio Inoki, (called by writer John Stravinsky "the dullest event in sports history"), Ali earned

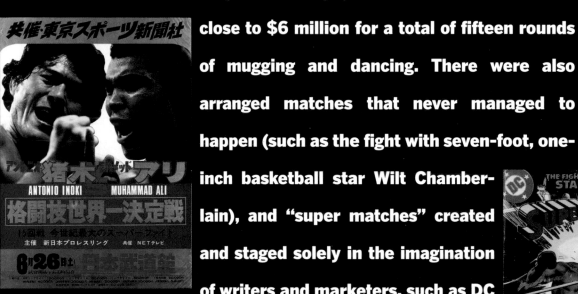

close to $6 million for a total of fifteen rounds of mugging and dancing. There were also arranged matches that never managed to happen (such as the fight with seven-foot, one-inch basketball star Wilt Chamber-lain), and "super matches" created and staged solely in the imagination of writers and marketers, such as DC

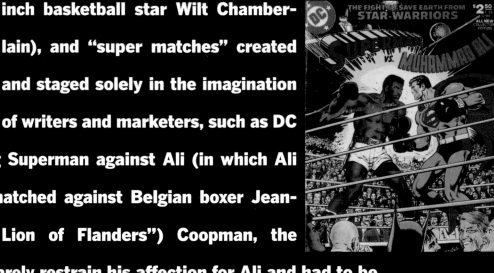

Comics' pitting Superman against Ali (in which Ali wins). When matched against Belgian boxer Jean-Pierre ("The Lion of Flanders") Coopman, the fighter could barely restrain his affection for Ali and had to be prevented from trying to kiss him at press conferences. The Belgian was so grateful to have the chance to box Ali that he celebrated by drinking champagne before the fight and between rounds.

circle, hand primed to hit him one more time, and never the need, a wholly intimate escort to the floor.

The referee took Ali to a corner. He stood there, he seemed lost in thought. Now he raced his feet in a quick but restrained shuffle as if to apologize for never asking his legs to dance, and looked on while Foreman tried to rouse himself.

Like a drunk hoping to get out of bed to go to work, Foreman rolled over, Foreman started the slow head-agonizing lift of all that foundered bulk God somehow gave him and whether he heard the count or no, was on his feet a fraction after the count of ten and whipped, for when Zack Clayton guided him with a hand at his back, he walked in docile steps to his corner and did not resist. Moore received him. Sadler received him.

"Feel all right?"

"Yeah," said Foreman.

"Well, don't worry. It's history now."

"Yeah."

"You're all right," said Sadler, "the rest will take care of itself."

In the ring Ali was seized by Rachman, by Gene Kilroy, by Bundini, by a host of Black friends old, new and very new, who charged up the aisles, leaped on the apron, sprang through the ropes and jumped near to touch him.

In the ring Ali fainted.

It occurred suddenly and without warning and almost no one saw it. Angelo Dundee circling the ropes to shout happy words at reporters was unaware of what had happened. So were all the smiling faces. It was only the eight or ten men immediately around him who knew. Those eight or ten mouths which had just been open in celebration now turned to grimaces of horror. Bundini went from laughing to weeping in five seconds.

Why Ali fainted, nobody might ever know. Whether it was a warning against excessive pride in years to come—one private bolt from Allah—or whether the weakness of sudden exhaustion, who could know? He was in any case too much

"And I want to be the first black champion got out that didn't get whipped.... Boxing's just a sport. They stand around and say 'Good fight, boy; you're a good boy; good goin'." And that's it. They don't look at fighters to have brains. They don't look at fighters to be businessmen, or humans, or intelligent. Fighters are just brutes that come to entertain the rich white people."

—Muhammad Ali

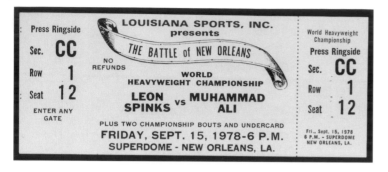

"The downfall of a great champion is sad to behold and it was with Muhammad Ali. On February 15, 1978, Ali lost his title on a fifteen-round decision to a novice fighter named Leon Spinks. Seven months later, he came back to challenge Spinks and capture the heavyweight championship for an unprecedented third time. Then after retiring from boxing, he returned again and suffered defeats · at the hands of Larry Holmes and Trevor Berbick. Those final fights did little to tarnish Ali's image, which had moved far beyond the ring, but they tarnished boxing. Ali today is a venerated public figure and deeply religious man who evokes feelings of love and respect throughout the world."

—Thomas Hauser

of a champion to allow an episode to arise, and was back on his feet before ten seconds were up.

David Frost was crying out: "Muhammad Ali has done it. The great man has done it. This is the most joyous scene ever seen in the history of boxing. This is an incredible scene. The place is going wild. Muhammad Ali has won." And because the announcer before him had picked the count up late and was two seconds behind the referee and so counting eight when Clayton said ten, it looked on all the closed circuit screens of the world as if Foreman had gotten up before the count was done, and confusion was everywhere. How could it be other? The media would always sprout the seed of confusion.

Then the rainy season, two weeks late, and packed with the frenzy of many an African atmosphere and many an unknown tribe, came at last to term with the waters of the cosmos and the groans of the Congo. The rainy season broke, and the stars of the African heaven came down. In the torrent, in that long protracted moon-green dawn, rain fell in silver sheets and silver blankets, waterfalls and rivers, in lakes that dropped like a stone from above, and with a slap of contact louder than the burst of fire in a forest....

> **Ali to a writer expressing surprise at Spinks' victory: "You're sitting down there ringside drinking beer and you're surprised? I was up in the ring getting my ass hit. You know I was surprised."**
>
> **— Muhammad Ali**

It poured onto the seats and poured through the aisles, it flowed down in jungle falls and streamed through the stairs and narrow entry halls, flooded the soccer field and washed beneath the ring carrying for its message the food and refuse of sixty thousand souls once sitting in the seats. Orange peels and fight tickets drifted into collection beneath the canvas, and batteries were drenched, generators gave out. Half the telex machines broke down in the storm, and the satellite ceased to send a picture or a word. What a debacle if the storm had come while the fight was on.

Ali would laugh next day and offer to take credit for holding back the rain.

LAS VEGAS H HILTON

presents

"THAT Championship Week!"

WEDNESDAY · FEB. 15
Doors open at 3 pm · Fights begin at 4 pm

WORLD HEAVYWEIGHT CHAMPIONSHIP
15 ROUNDS

MUHAMMAD ALI vs LEON SPINKS

CHICAGO, ILL. · CHAMPION ST. LOUIS, MO. · CHALLENGER

PROMOTED IN ASSOCIATION WITH TOP RANK, INC. · MATCHMAKER , MEL GREB

WBA LIGHT-HEAVYWEIGHT CHAMPIONSHIP
15 ROUNDS

VICTOR GALINDEZ vs JESSE BURNETT
Argentina · Champion Los Angeles, Calif. · Challenger

PROMOTED IN ASSOCIATION WITH TOP RANK, INC. AND RUDOLPHO SABBATINI · MATCHMAKER, LORENZO SPAGNOLI

WBC FEATHERWEIGHT CHAMPIONSHIP
15 ROUNDS

DANNY 'Little Red' LOPEZ vs DAVID 'Poison' KOTEY
Los Angeles, Calif. · Champion Ghana · Challenger

PROMOTED IN ASSOCIATION WITH TOP RANK, INC. AND AILEEN EATON, INC. · MATCHMAKER, DON CHARGIN

...PLUS TWO 10 ROUNDERS

SATURDAY · FEB. 11
Doors open at 11 am · Fights begin at 12 noon

WBC WELTERWEIGHT CHAMPIONSHIP
15 ROUNDS

CARLOS PALOMINO vs RYU SORIMACHI
Los Angeles, Calif. · Champion Tokyo · Challenger

PROMOTED IN ASSOCIATION WITH TOP RANK, INC. AND AILEEN EATON, INC. · MATCHMAKER, DON CHARGIN

...PLUS ALL-STAR UNDERCARD

FEB. 15 CARD	RINGSIDES $200. GRANDSTANDS $200. $100. $50.

FEB. 11 CARD	RINGSIDES $20. GRANDSTANDS $20. $15. $10.

TICKETS ON SALE AT HILTON PAVILION

FOR TICKETS & INFORMATION CALL (702) 732-8817

BOX OFFICE OPEN 10 AM TO 6 PM DAILY

CBS·TV LIVE FEB. 15 & FEB. 11

HILTON PAVILION

TOTAL SOUTHERN NEVADA BLACKOUT

"Of all the fights I lost in boxing, losing to Spinks hurt the most. That's because it was my own fault.... I just couldn't leave boxing that way; losing an embarrassing fight like that."

— Muhammad Ali

1980s by Joyce Carol Oates

After his retirement, against the advice of friends, Ali climbed back in the ring in 1980 to fight Larry Holmes. He called Holmes "The Peanut," "because his head is shaped like a peanut and I'm going to shell him and send him to Plains, Georgia."

The Last Fights
Hard Victories, Irreversible Loss

Muhammad Ali, born Cassius Marcellus Clay in Louisville, Kentucky, on January 17, 1942, grandson of a slave, began boxing at the age of twelve, and, by eighteen, had fought one hundred and eight amateur bouts. How is it possible, the young man who, in his twenties, would astonish the world not just with the brilliance of his boxing but the sharpness of his wit, seemed to have been a dull-average student in high school who graduated 376th out of a class of 391; in 1966, his score on a mental aptitude test was an Army I.Q. of 78, well below military qualification. In 1975, Ali confessed to a reporter that he "can't read too good" and had not read ten pages of all the material written about him. I remember the television interview in which, asked what else he might have done with his life, Ali paused, for several seconds, clearly not knowing how to reply. All he'd ever known, he said finally, was boxing.

> "It happened to all of them. It happened to Joe Louis, Sugar Ray Robinson, and Willie Pep. It happened to Archie Moore, Rocky Graziano, and Carlos Ortiz. I know; it happened to me. Call it age. Call it growing old. Call it the erosion of time."
>
> —Jose Torres

"Why does man go to the moon? I say, because it's there. Why did those blind people climb up that mountain? Because it was there. Why am I fighting for the title for the fourth time? Because it's there. No man but me has ever won it three times. No man has ever had the chance to do it four times." **—Muhammad Ali**

Mental aptitude tests cannot measure genius except in certain narrow ranges, and the genius of the body, the play of lightning-swift reflexes coupled with unwavering precision and confidence, eludes comprehension. All great boxers possess this genius, which scrupulous training hones, but can never create. "Styles make fights," as Ali's great trainer Angelo Dundee says, and "style" was young Ali's trademark. Yet even after early wins over such veterans as Archie Moore and Henry Cooper, the idiosyncrasies of Ali's style aroused skepticism in boxing experts. After winning the Olympic gold medal in 1960, Ali was described by A.J. Leibling as "skittering. . . like a pebble over water." Everyone could see that this brash young boxer held his hands too low; he leaned away from punches instead of properly slipping them; his jab was light and flicking; he seemed to be perpetually on the brink of disaster. As a seven-to-one underdog in his first title fight with Sonny Liston, the twenty-two-year-old challenger astounded the experts with his performance, which was like none other they had ever seen in the heavyweight division; he so outboxed and demoralized Liston that Liston "quit on his stool" after the sixth round. A new era in boxing had begun, like a new music.

> "Ali rode the crest of a new wave of athletes—competitors who were both big and fast. . . . Ali had a combination of size and speed that had never been seen in a fighter before, along with incredible will and courage. He also brought a new style to boxing. Jack Dempsey changed fisticuffs from a kind where fighters fought in a tense defensive style to a wild sensual assault. Ali revolutionized boxing the way black basketball players have changed basketball today. He changed what happened in the ring, and elevated it to a level that was previously unknown."
>
> —Larry Merchant

In the context of contemporary boxing—the sport is in one of its periodic slumps—there is nothing more instructive and rejuvenating than to see again these old, early fights of Ali's, when, as his happy boast had it, he floated like a

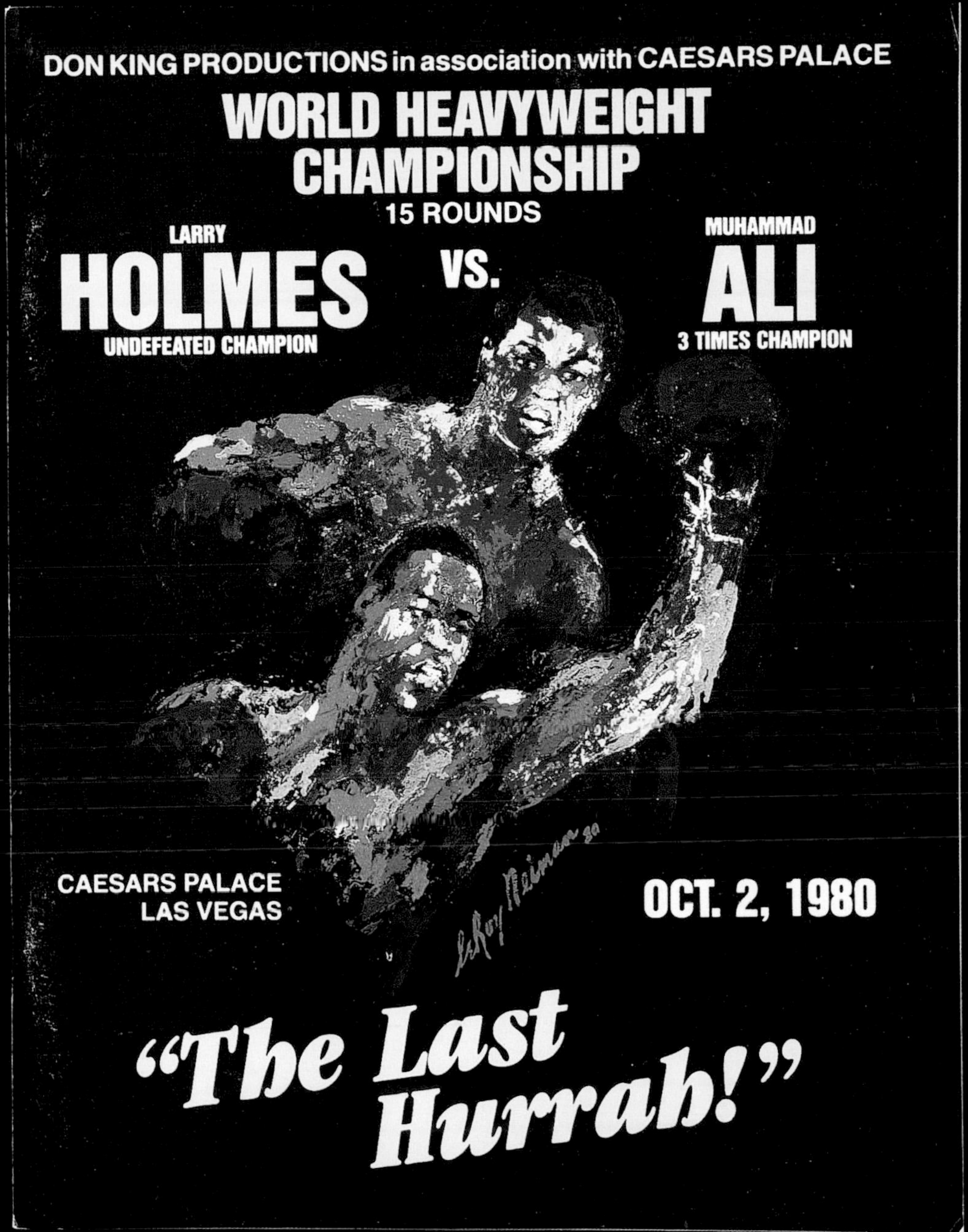

DON KING PRODUCTIONS in association with CAESARS PALACE

WORLD HEAVYWEIGHT CHAMPIONSHIP
15 ROUNDS

LARRY
HOLMES
UNDEFEATED CHAMPION

VS.

MUHAMMAD
ALI
3 TIMES CHAMPION

CAESARS PALACE
LAS VEGAS

OCT. 2, 1980

"The Last Hurrah!"

"Ali, down to his graying hairs, skillfully conned many into believing he had a chance. With another torturous training schedule, he lost forty pounds of mostly belly fat and impressed camp visitors with his physique—never mind that much of his weight-loss owed to amphetamines that would drain his energy. But most damaging of all was an apparently incorrect diagnosis that Ali had a thyroid condition. A doctor prescribed one tablet of Thyrolar, a potentially lethal drug, and to make matters worse, Ali took three tablets instead of the one prescribed. The combination of age, ill effects from the drugs, and a sprightly and talented Larry Holmes left Ali with virtually no chance."

—John Stravinsky

Ali-Holmes

butterfly and stung like a bee and threw punches faster than opponents could see—like the "mystery" right to the temple of Liston that felled him, in the first minute of the first round of their rematch. These early fights, the most brilliant being against Cleveland Williams, in 1966, predate by a decade the long, grueling, punishing fights of Ali's later career whose cumulative effects hurt Ali so irrevocably, resulting in what doctors call, carefully, his "Parkinsonianism"—to distinguish it from "Parkinson's Disease." There is a true visceral shock in observing a heavyweight with the grace, agility, swiftness of hands and feet, defensive skills and ring cunning of a middleweight Ray Robinson, or a lightweight Willie Pep!—like all great athletes, Ali has to be seen to be believed.

In a secular, yet pseudo-religious and sentimental nation like the United States, it is quite natural that sports stars emerge as "heroes"—"legends"—"icons." Who else? George Santayana described religion as "another world to live in" and no world is so *other*, so set off from the disorganization and disenchantment of the quotidian than the world, or worlds, of sports. [We witnessed] the transformation of the birth of Ali out of the unexpectedly stubborn and idealistic will of young Cassius Clay: how, immediately following his first victory over Liston, he declared himself a convert to the Nation of Islam (more popularly known as the Black Muslims) and "no longer a Christian." He repudiated his "slave name" of Cassius Clay to become Muhammad Ali. (A name which, incidentally, the *New York Times*, among other censorious white publications, would not honor through the 1960s.) Ali became, virtually overnight, a spokesman for black America as no other athlete, certainly not the purposefully reticent Joe Louis, had ever done—"I don't have to be what you want me to be," he told white, media-

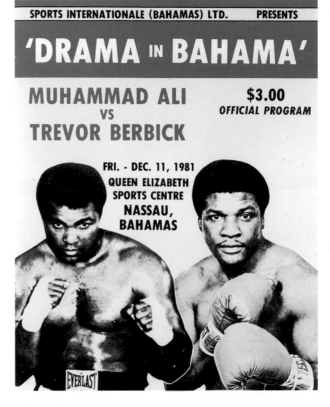

SPORTS INTERNATIONALE (BAHAMAS) LTD.   PRESENTS

'DRAMA IN BAHAMA'

MUHAMMAD ALI
VS
TREVOR BERBICK

$3.00
OFFICIAL PROGRAM

FRI. - DEC. 11, 1981
QUEEN ELIZABETH
SPORTS CENTRE
NASSAU,
BAHAMAS

EVERLAST

> I'd be the biggest fool in the world to go out a loser after being the first three-time champ. None of the black athletes before me ever got out when they were on top. My people need one black man to come out on top. I've got to be the first.
>
> —Muhammad Ali

After his loss to Holmes, Ali was matched with Trevor Berbick in 1981. Before the fight he crowed: "Forty is fun, because life has just begun. Age is mind over matter—as long as you don't mind, it don't matter." Ali was beaten in ten rounds; it would be his last fight. Afterward, he admitted: "I was slow. I was weak. Nothing but Father Time. I know it's the end."

Ali announced his Parkinson's diagnosis at a 1986 press conference. In the announcement, he reminded his audience: "I'm still lookin' pretty."

dominated America, "I'm free to be what I want to be." Two years later, refusing to be inducted into the army to fight in Vietnam, Ali, beleaguered by reporters, uttered one of the great, incendiary remarks of that era: "Man, I ain't got no quarrel with them Vietcong."

How ingloriously white America responded to Ali, how unashamedly racist and punitive: the government retaliated by overruling a judge who had granted Ali the status of conscientious objector, fined him $10,000 and sentenced him to five years in prison; outrageously, he was stripped of his heavyweight title and deprived of his license to box. Eventually, the U.S. Supreme Court would overturn the conviction, and, as the tide of opinion shifted in the country, in the early 1970s as the Vietnam War wound down, Ali returned triumphantly to boxing again, and regained the heavyweight title not once but twice. Years of exile during which he'd endured the angry self-righteousness of the conservative white press seemed, wonderfully, not to have embittered him. He had become a hero. He had entered myth.

Yet the elegiac title of Angelo Dundee's chapter in Dave Anderson's *In The Corner*—"We Never Saw Muhammad Ali at His Best"—defines the nature of Ali's sacrifice for his principles, and the loss to boxing. When, after the three-and-a-half-year layoff, Ali returned to the ring, he was of course no longer the seemingly invincible boxer he'd been; he'd lost his legs, thus his primary line of defense. Like the maturing writer who learns to replace

"He was seen by everybody as one of their own. The heavyweight champion of the world beats people up, but when you were near him, you never felt fear."

—Kareem Abdul-Jabbar

the incandescent head-on energies of youth with what is called technique, Ali would have to descend into his physical being and experience for the first time the punishment ("the nearest thing to death"); this is the lot of the great boxer willing to put himself to the test. As Ali's personal physician at that time, Ferdie Pacheco, said, "[Ali] discovered something which was both very good and very bad. Very bad in that it led to the physical damage he suffered later in his career; very good in that it eventually got him back the championship. He discovered that he could take a punch."

The secret of Ali's mature success, and the secret of his tragedy: *he could take a punch.*

For the remainder of his twenty-year career, Muhammad Ali took punches, many of the kind that, delivered to a non-boxer, would kill him or her outright—from Joe Frazier in their three exhausting marathon bouts, from George Foreman, from Ken Norton, Leon Spinks, Larry Holmes. Where in his feckless youth Ali was a dazzling figure combining, say, the brashness of Hotspur and the insouciance of Lear's Fool, he became in these dark, brooding, increasingly willed fights the closest analogue boxing contains to Lear himself; or, rather, since there is no great fight without two great boxers, the title matches Ali-Frazier I (which Frazier won by a decision) and Ali-Frazier III (which Ali won, just barely, when Frazier virtually collapsed after the fourteenth round) are boxing's analogues to *King Lear*—ordeals of unfathomable human courage and resilience raised to the level of classic tragedy. These somber and terrifying boxing matches make us weep for their very futility; we seem to be in the presence of human experience too profound to be named—beyond the syntactical strategies and diminishments of language. The mystic's dark night of the soul, transmogrified as a brutal meditation of the body.

And Ali-Foreman, Zaire, 1974: the occasion of the infamous "rope-a-dope" defense, by which the thirty-two-year-old Ali exhausted his twenty-six-year-old opponent by the inspired method of, simply, and horribly, allowing him to punch himself out on Ali's body and arms. This is a fight of such a magical quality that even to watch it closely is not to see how it was done, its fairy tale reversal in the eighth round executed. (One of Norman Mailer's most impassioned books, *The Fight*, is about this fight; watching a tape of Ali on the

"I've got to have Parkinson's syndrome. If I was in perfect health, people would be afraid of me. They thought I was Superman. Now they can go, 'He's human, like us.'"

—Muhammad Ali

"'See that? See me?' Ali sat in an overstuffed chair watching himself on the television screen. The voice came in a swallowed whisper and his finger waggled as it pointed toward his younger self. . . . 'That's the only time I was scared in the ring,' Ali said. 'Sonny Liston. First time. First round. Said he was going to kill me'. . . . Ali smiled. With great effort, he smiled. Parkinson's is a disease of the nervous system that stiffens the muscles and freezes the face into a stolid mask. Motor control degenerates. Speech degenerates. . . . Ali still walked well. He was still powerful in the arms and across the chest It was obvious, just from shaking his hand, that he still possessed a knockout punch. No, for him the special torture was speech and expression, as if the disease intended to strike first at what had once pleased him, and pleased (or annoyed) the world, most. . . . Ali was smiling now as his younger self, Cassius Clay, flicked a nasty left jab into Liston's brow. 'You watchin' this? Sooo fast! Sooo pretty!'"

ropes enticing, and infuriating, and frustrating, and finally exhausting his opponent by an offense in the guise of a defense, I pondered what sly lessons of masochism Mailer absorbed from being at ringside that day, what deep-imprinted resolve to outwear all adversaries.)

These hard-won victories began irreversible loss: progressive deterioration of Ali's kidneys, hands, reflexes, stamina. By the time of that most depressing of modern-day matches, Ali-Holmes, 1980, when Ali was thirty-eight years old, Ferdie Pacheco had long departed the

> "Parkinson's disease has made him a more spiritual person. Muhammad believes God gave it to him to bring him to another level, to create another destiny."

Ali camp, dismissed for having advised Ali to retire; those who supported Ali's decision to fight, like the bout's promoter Don King, had questionable motives. It is a wonder that Ali survived this fight at all: the fight was, in Sylvester Stallone's words, "like watching an autopsy on a man who's still alive." (In *The Black Lights*, Thomas Hauser describes the bedlam that followed this vicious fight at Caesar's Palace, Las Vegas, where gamblers plunged in an orgy of gambling, as in a frenzy of feeding, or copulation: "Ali and Holmes had done their job.") Incredibly, Ali was allowed to fight once more, with Trevor Berbick, in December 1981, before retiring permanently.

The brash rap-style egoism of young Cassius Clay underwent a considerable transformation during Ali's long public career, yet strikes us, perhaps, as altered only in tone: "Boxing was just to introduce me to the world," Ali has told his biographer. Mystically involved in the Nation of Islam, Ali sincerely believes himself an international emissary for peace, love, and understanding (he who once wreaked such violence upon his opponents!); and who is to presume to feel sorry for one who will not feel sorry for himself?

In 1986, Muhammad married Lonnie Williams, who had been a fan since she was a child. She remembers it clearly: "Right before he fought Sonny Liston, which would have been when I was seven, he came to town with a big bus. It had a loudspeaker system and was painted different colors with the name 'Cassius Clay' on the side. He put as many kids as he could on the bus, and we drove all over town. He'd shout out, 'Who's the greatest?' And we'd shout back, 'You are!'.... What happened was, our friendship became very strong, which is the way I think all marriages should start; because if two people aren't friends, I don't see how they can be in love. We knew we wanted to be together...."

1990s
by Peter Richmond

"This afflicted man—who made his name by fighting and whose espousal of the Nation of Islam religion and refusal to enter the military draft during the Vietnam War made him a symbol of division—offers himself up now as a vehicle for worldwide healing."

—William Plummer

In Excelsis
Finally, The Greatest

On the table

in front of him sit a copy of the holy Koran and a plate holding three frosted raspberry coffee cakes, and when he leans forward on the couch and reaches out it is not for enlightenment. It is for a piece of pastry. With his right hand wobbling just this side of uncontrollably, he guides it, slow inch by slow inch, toward the mouth that once yapped without stopping but that now, largely mute, chews slowly, as the eyes stare straight ahead, seeing nothing; only the patter of a cold rain splashing the leaves of the trees outside the window mars the silence. Flecks of frosting tumble in slow motion to light on his belly, which gently swells beneath a black sweater. I am sitting next to him. Close enough to see the tiny scar on his eyelid that looks like a birthmark. Close enough to hear him chew. Close enough to taste the cake as he tastes it. The look on his face is the fat and happy near smile

"I've seen the whole world. I learned somethin' from people everywhere. There's truth in Hinduism, Christianity, Islam, all religions. And in just plain talkin'. The only religion that matters is the real religion— love." —Muhammad Ali

> **"Ali's hold on the public is incredible. No one in the world is more loved. I was in Atlantic City the morning after one of Mike Tyson's fights. I was in the hotel restaurant, when all of the sudden I heard someone applaud. Then more people applauded, and began to stand up. It was Muhammad Ali coming into the room and I got goosebumps from what I saw."**
>
> **—Jose Torres**

topping the fat and happy body of all the renderings of Buddha you've ever seen. It is an expression of bemusement and contentment and wonder at the beauty to be found in the simplest things.

As I watch him eat, I have never been more sure of a man's inner contentment. Except maybe when he eats the second piece.

It's not supposed to be Buddha. It's supposed to be Allah, because it is Allah who has ruled his life since even before Liston, and Allah who controls it now more than ever before. The contents of his briefcase say so. He is carrying the briefcase as he enters the room, so still even in walking that he does not disturb the air around him. He opens the briefcase to reveal hundreds of well-thumbed sheets of paper filled with type-written words. It is the briefcase a man would carry if he were to knock on your screen door to convert you to his faith, and on this day, dressed in black, shoulders slumping toward his paunch, gray sprinkling his temples, he looks like such a man.... His briefcase also holds a black-and-white photograph of three boxers—Ali, Joe Louis, and Sugar Ray Robinson; it looks like a snapshot from the turn of the century—but most of the case's contents are there to do Allah's work.

It's easiest for him to talk about Allah, although it is not easy for him to talk, because the muscles of his face don't work as well as they once did. His wife, Lonnie, has asked if I want her to sit with us so she can tell me what he is saying. Lonnie is a strong woman who walks through a room like a beautiful storm approaching. But right now I ask her if Ali and I can be alone and if she could close the door, which she does, leaving the two of us in silence in a small room in the suite of offices on Ali's southern Michigan farm. The farm used to belong to Al Capone's bookmaker. A workman doing renovations recently dug some bullets out of the floorboards from back in the days when people were shooting one another here. Now it's just about the quietest place on earth.

After he hands me several more tracts, I tell him I'm pretty much a nonbeliever, and at this his eyebrows arch up and the words come quickly.

"Do you believe that phone made itself?"

No, I say.

"Do you believe the chair made itself?"

No.

"Do you believe the table made itself?"

No.

"Do you believe the sun made itself?"

No.

"The Supreme Being made it...."

It has taken me a full hour in his presence to begin to recognize the nuances in his shaking fingers, and it has taken me equally long to understand the nuances of his facial expressions, from the eyebrows shooting straight up in true surprise to the rare half smile to the flat, expressionless expressions that are differentiated by the degree to which the eyes and the eyelids move.

All the gyrations and the mugging and the shouting have been distilled into a thimbleful of expressions, but it is a bottomless thimble. So when with a single slight crook of an index finger he tells me not to help him, it's as if a healthy person had slapped my hand away. Then he tries again, rocks against the back of the couch and vaults himself up. He walks over to a corner of the room, where he turns away and, with his back to me, slowly rises off his feet.

His body appears to levitate—his left foot is off the ground. I cannot see his right foot. Maybe he *is* levitating. This sounds absurd, but it would make more sense if you were in the room with him and could feel the otherworldliness his utter stillness and oddly detached gaze now impart. In the lasting silences between long questions and short answers and magic tricks, as he stares straight ahead, I begin to feel a mounting sense of disorientation. It's as if the room is growing smaller or he is growing bigger, as if the space is too little to hold whatever he is becoming now. It's as if Euclidean rules are being bent.

I'd expected the disease to have robbed him of the vitality that once exploded from him. I'd expected the disease to

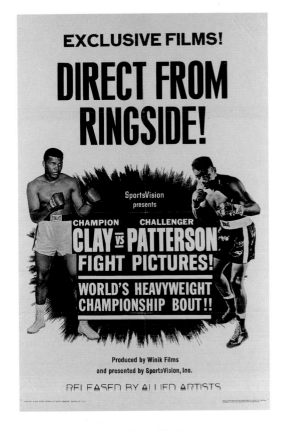

"I came to love Ali. I came to see that I was a fighter and he was history."

—Floyd Patterson

"I still envy him. He has something

I have never been able to attain and

very few people I know possess. He

has an absolute and sincere faith."

—Bill Russell

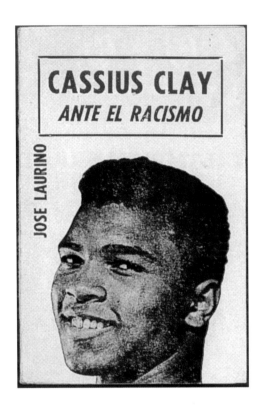

JOSE LAURINO

CASSIUS CLAY
ANTE EL RACISMO

"I never talk about boxing. It's just something I did. It served its purpose. I was only about eleven, twelve years old—I saw Negroes being hung, a boy named Emmett Till, castrated and burned up. I said I'm gonna get famous so I can help my people—that was my intention." —**Muhammad Ali**

represent the ultimate cruel triumph of the world that had always wanted the black boy from Louisville, Kentucky, to shut the hell up.

But up close, I am discovering that his affliction has taken nothing away, none of the energy, none of the wit, none of the pride; it has only bound all of it, captured and constricted it, with the entirely unexpected result that, as an aeon of geologic forces can compress a large vein of coal into a very small diamond, whatever was the essence of Muhammad Ali is now somehow magnified. He is at last what he always pretended to be but never was: the Greatest. For it must be axiomatic that if someone calls himself the Greatest, as Ali did for years, he cannot possibly be; the Greatest would never have to label himself as such. Only when he was forced to stop proclaiming his greatness did it become possible. . . .

That night 11,000 people filled Freedom Hall at the fairgrounds to see an entertainment-extravaganza tribute to Muhammad Ali. After the gospel choir sang, a boxing ring was wheeled to the front of the stage and a series of embarrassing boxing exhibitions ensued as an expressionless Ali watched from a mezzanine seat.

Then a thirteen-year-old boy bounced into the ring—a thin kid with gloves as big as his head, his face, nearly in shadow, framed in the padding of the protective headgear. But I could see the eyes and the mouth; they were the features of a boxer before a fight. It turned out he was the youth boxing champion of South Carolina, and he was going to fight Muhammad Ali. I do not think that the youth boxing champion of South Carolina had the slightest idea of the significance of the man who was going to join him in the ring.

I glanced at a man seated next to me, and the look he cast back mirrored the anxiety in my eyes. Then someone raised the ropes for Ali, and as he slowly ducked to climb into the ring the applause swelled, but it was a worried ovation. The bell rang, and the kid charged, fists flying out like misdirected darts; he wanted to kill the old fool. But before anyone could wince, Ali was dancing to one side and then dancing back the other way—not the Ali of 1965, but not a cripple either: It was the dance of an overweight former athlete who was perfectly healthy. The kid could not land a punch.

Then, as the cheers of relief started to rise, he did the Ali shuffle. I'd forgotten about the Ali shuffle. This was not the shuffle of 1966 but the shuffle of an overweight former athlete in perfect health. Ali did not do one dance and one shuffle. He kept it up for a full minute.

Finally, he reached down and grabbed the kid in a bear hug and smiled the best smile he could, although it was just a wink of a smile, and that was the end of it.

When I found him a few minutes later in a room behind the stage, dining on fried chicken, he did not resemble the man in the boxing ring, except for the face. He was surrounded by friends and family, and women—one was fetching him a piece of cake. There was an inordinate number of women in the room, watching him avail himself of the post event spread, making sure he got enough to eat, wearing expressions that seemed quite maternal. They were not the expressions I'd seen on the women at the black-tie banquet the night before. After Louisville's high society had grazed its way through a two-hour open-bar cocktail party, Ali had slowly made his way to the dais, and I saw on the faces of the pearled women with low-cut gowns and bustiered girls in impossibly high heels the distinct expression I've come to recognize as the one women wear when they're looking at a man they want.

The boxing match was the last official event of Muhammad Ali's weekend, but the last unofficial event took place at midnight in the bar at the Seelbach Hotel. It is a historic place, often cited in those stories about great old bars in the great Old South. Natalie Cole and her band were lounging at the bar. I was with one of Ali's counsel and her boyfriend when Howard Bingham, sloe-eyed and cool, slid a chair up to our table and ordered a beer. Bingham, a photographer, has been by Ali's side from the beginning, and he is the only one who never left it.

I waited until Howard was halfway through his beer before

"Today . . . he is as loved and embraced as he once was scorned and despised."

—William Nack

105

I asked him what had happened at Freedom Hall that evening.

"What do you mean?" he asked.

The dancing, I said. The shuffling.

"Oh yeah, he can do that; he does that sometimes."

He can? Then why doesn't he do it more often?

Bingham had no immediate answer. He was not looking at me or at anything when a moment later he took his right arm and started to windmill it, like an old Ali punch. Then he stopped, and the hand wrapped around the mug of beer.

"Sometimes," Bingham said, "I just want to..." But he did not finish the sentence. He said something else: "He could be 100 percent better."

And he could. If he spent more time in boxing rings. It turns out that only when Muhammad Ali is in a boxing ring can he, or does he choose to, turn back the clock. It's only a boxing ring, fittingly enough, that moves him to movement. Perhaps he believes that if some of us are now finding divine inspiration in his metaphysical majesty, his real power will always derive from his ability to outwit, outpunch and overpower everyone else.

What Parkinson's disease does is make you brittle. Ali's version of the disease is a slow one, but it's making him brittle nonetheless. The way to fight being brittle—to keep the disease at bay—is to work at being limber. And the only time he feels like working at being limber—at fighting the disease—is when he's in an environment where he's always been accustomed to fighting.

"He won't exercise in a regular gym or do the Nautilus or a StairMaster; he will not do it," says Lonnie. Her voice is exasperated, because she is exasperated. "I have bought him state-of-the-art equipment. He won't use it. He says it's for sissies. That's why I'm building him a gym on the farm, with a ring and mirrors and a heavy bag. Because that's what he knows. And that's how he wants to do it.

"Sometimes Muhammad, unfortunately, might use this illness. Don't get me wrong, but Muhammad knows when to turn it on and off. And sometimes I think he does it

"[Ali] and Howard Bingham are the best of pals, the Damon and Pythias of our time. They have loved each other for thirty-five and a half years, through thick and thin, championships and marriages and children; through their lives, across our time."

So, a few days later, in another place, Ali smiles, looking across the room to Bingham, and behind the trembling hands and the flaccid face, there is a glint in his eyes that suddenly shines from a time the world lay at his feet and he was as healthy and handsome as God ever made one man. But never mind that. It's O.K. "I'm lucky," Ali mumbles. "Did you ever have a good friend?"

—Frank Deford

deliberately. Turns it off. He's a master manipulator; I'm not going to kid you. He will look more fragile than he actually is. Why he does it, I don't know."

Perhaps I do. Perhaps if I were being worshiped by flocks of followers, my every whim attended to, and all I could see from behind the smoked glass was legions shouting my name and feeding me cake, well, I would have stopped trying to get better a long time ago, too. Especially if the crowds were finally affirming what I'd been saying for forty years: that in me you see a god.

"I began to suspect that he was a special vessel that might be ordained for special things," a writer named Mort Sharnik once said of Cassius Clay as the writer tried to come to grips with the essence of this strange new champion. "*Esse est percipi*," an eighteenth-century bishop named George Berkeley said many years earlier as he tried to figure out what it meant to exist, to be. After a lifetime of considering the notion, Berkeley decided that to be is to be perceived. And so it must be now with Muhammad Ali. If he is a vessel, it is not only his own self that fills it; it is filled up by all of us, filled with whatever it is we need to find in him. He is what we perceive him to be.

What we see in him is purely an individual matter. It might be something in the eyes, which seem particularly expressive because everything else on the face has shut down—a sense in his eyes of not only the playful jester but also the kind and compassionate man whose clowning and belittling of opponents often obscured the goodness of the soul within. It might be forgiveness: of him, for adopting a racist religion or acting like a self-centered showman at so many people's expense—like the cruelty he showered on Joe Frazier ("See how ignorant you are?"); or forgiveness of ourselves, for not realizing how special he was beneath the bluster and the lunacy. For not sensing what we had in our midst.

It might be reverence for the physical embodiment of the greatest man ever to fight, and for the greatest athlete we've ever known: The title of heavyweight champion, before its devaluation, was a kingly title. And no one has ever ruled the

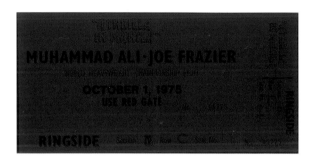

"I hated Ali. I'd like to fight Ali-Clay-whatever-his-name-is again tomorrow. Twenty years I've been fighting Ali, and I still want to take him apart and send him back to Jesus."   —Joe Frazier

sport as gracefully, or as magically—although his crowning triumph, his victory over Frazier in their third fight, in Manila, was the most brutally beautiful heavyweight-championship fight in history, a battle won not with wits but with soul. If the disease came on while he was fighting—if it was not inherited, as his wife insists—then this is the fight during which it must have taken root.

It might be simple awe at the survival of a man who had the balls to stand up to white America and risk its wrath when most of us would have shut up and joined the damned army. In 1967 to be a young black man from Kentucky who refused induction—one year before Martin Luther King Jr. was shot in Memphis, three years after three civil rights workers were murdered in Mississippi—was to be made of a singular fabric.

And it might be pity, although if it's pity, he neither merits it nor wants it. When I ask him if we should feel sorry for him, he says, "No," and slumps back against the couch in a manner that I recognize as meaning he will have more to say on the matter in a moment. This happens only three times in our two hours in that room: There are three questions he wants to answer slowly, not reflexively. This is not to say that some of his quick answers aren't honest ones. When I ask if he misses boxing and he quickly answers, "No"; when I ask if he'd want his son to be a boxer and he quickly says, "No"; when I ask, "Are you a happy man?" and he quickly answers, "Um-hmm." But three times when I ask him questions, he slumps back on the couch and closes his eyes, then opens them and speaks.

Sometimes he gets only the first three or four words out and then has to stop and try again before uttering a complete thought—like a car turning over several times before catching on a cold morning.

So when I ask if we should feel sorry for him, he says, "No," and then a few moments later he says, "Everything ... everything ... everything has a purpose."

Another time I ask if he'd change anything in his life.

"Ali spreads the message that more of us need to know: 'I am the greatest,' he says. Not that Negroes think they are greater than anyone else. But I want them to know that they are just as great as any other human being alive."

—Jackie Robinson

"A couple of flies did midair imitations of the Ali shuffle as the original, Muhammad Ali himself, sat in the motel lobby talking with a companion. One fly alighted on the right knee of Ali. 'See that fly? Mind that fly,' said Ali, his conversational tone interrupted by his whisper. His large left hand began to creep out. His eyes were fixed on the fly. 'You gotta know how to do it,' he said, barely moving his lips. 'The fly is facing me and he can only fly forward. Now I come forward and turn my hand backhanded. It's like a left jab.' Ali struck. Then he brought his fist in front of the man seated next to him. He slowly opened his hand. Ali looked up wide-eyed. 'Thought I had him,' he said. 'My timing's off.'"

—Ira Berkow

After several seconds, he says, "I wouldn't change nothin'. It all turned out to be good."

The third time, I ask how he wants history to remember him. This is the one he takes the most time to think about. He closes his eyes and slumps against the back of the couch for what seems to be a very long time. Then he opens his eyes, leans forward and says in quick bursts of words, "I want people to say, 'He fought for his rights. Fought for my people. Most famous black man in the world. Strong believer in God.'"

He does not say, "I was the Greatest." He never says anything like it.

I have a million more questions, but he is tired, and I am not going to get the answers I want. When I ask what lessons he has learned on his long and troublesome journey—when I lean in and, in tones drenched with meaning, ask him what we should *know*—he says, "Do a lot of running eat the right foods."

We shake hands—it's a soft handshake but not a sickly one; it's like a gentleman's handshake—and he picks up the briefcase and rises to walk down the hall to say good-bye to his wife, who is working in another room, before he walks over to the main house. I take a tour of the rest of the office suite. One room's windows overlook an expanse of emerald green grass bordering a river, and stacked against the wall beneath the windows are thirteen translucent plastic cartons with the words PROPERTY OF THE U.S. POSTAL SERVICE printed on the sides. Each is overflowing with letters and envelopes. Perhaps a thousand pieces of mail.

"A week's worth," says a woman whose job is to open them and answer them: the well-wishers, the autograph requesters, the charity seekers. Most of Ali's life is given over to good works now. Last fall a Roman Catholic nun who cares for Liberian children at a missionary center in the Ivory Coast wrote Ali to ask for his help. The next month, she was surprised to see him there in person, giving out food.

In another room sits a woman who presides over the memorabilia being packed up to be shipped to the nascent Ali

"Ali was by far the most interesting athlete of my generation. Some came close: Bill Russell, Joe Namath, Willie Mays. But Ali was electrifying when he was at his best and champion. He towered above everyone else. I remember the discouragement I felt, and others felt, that we hadn't done enough for this extraordinary man when his title was taken away from him. Of course, he won vindication in the courts, but that wasn't enough. He had to get his title back, and that had to be done in the ring. . . .

"Even today, when I think about Ali, I smile, and there aren't many people who have that effect. There was an aura about him. He glowed, sort of a strange golden color; like some statue bronzed gold. He shone as though he was possessed of some wonderful power that his skin just couldn't contain."

—George Plimpton

museum in Louisville: the autographed Golden Gloves, the photograph of Ali standing over Liston's prone body in Lewiston, shouting at his defeated foe. Glass trophies and engraved plaques line walls, huddle atop tables, rest on floors—too many to examine any particular honor; the cumulative effect of the glittery clutter says enough.

My tour has taken ten or fifteen minutes, and as I turn down the hallway toward the door that will take me outside, I see that Ali is standing exactly where I saw him last; he hasn't moved an inch. He is standing in a doorway looking at his wife, who is sitting in front of a computer wearing a telephone headset. She is a woman with discernible soft and humorous sides, but she is also a no-nonsense person, and right now she is talking to a lawyer in tones as authoritative and sure as those of a general commanding troop placement from a bunker, discussing some award Ali will be receiving in New York next month; she is running the business of Muhammad Ali.

He leans down to whisper something in my ear. By now I know not to expect anything profound.

"I like my office," he says, and I nod, understanding instantly what he means. That he likes standing and watching people testify to his power and his goodness. That he likes all these tangible testaments to how important he has become. Also, I think he likes the women.

He escorts me down the stairs, out the door, and we stand for a moment beneath the outstretched arms of the giant elms. This is where I leave him, surveying his kingdom. As I walk to my car, he is still standing there, and as I drive away down the long, winding driveway toward the iron gates, I have no doubt that as soon as I'm out of sight he will turn around and go back upstairs to eat the last piece of coffee cake.

"Everything I do, I say to myself, 'Will God accept this?' Sleep is a rehearsal for death. One day you wake up and it's judgment day. So you do good deeds. I love sick people. I love to go to hospitals. I don't worry about disease. Allah will protect me. He always does."

—Muhammad Ali

"[Boxing's] dyin'. I always said it would die when I left. Just look at it—there's Holyfield, there used to be Tyson. But there's no Muhammad Ali, no kind of hero."

—Muhammad Ali

113

"I'll tell you how I'd like to be remembered: as a black man who won the heavyweight title and who was humorous and who treated everyone right. As a man who never looked down on those who looked up to him and who helped as many of his people as he could—financially and also in their fight for freedom, justice and equality. As a man who wouldn't hurt his people's dignity by doing something that would embarrass them. As a man who tried to unite his people through the faith of Islam. If that's asking too much, then I guess I'd settle for being remembered only as a great boxer who became a preacher and a champion of his people. And I wouldn't even mind if folks forgot how pretty I was."

The Fights

A Chronology 1960-1981

1960

October 29, 1960
vs. Tunney Hunsaker
Freedom Hall
Louisville, Kentucky
Won in 6

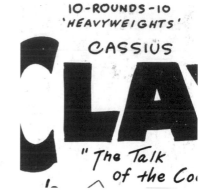

December 27, 1960
vs. Herb Siler
Auditorium
Miami Beach, Florida
Won, KO in 4

1961

January 17, 1961
vs. Tony Esperti
Auditorium
Miami Beach, Florida
Won, KO in 3

June 26, 1961
vs. Duke Sabedong
Convention Center
Las Vegas, Nevada
Won in 10

July 22, 1961
vs. Alonzo Johnson
Freedom Hall
Louisville, Kentucky
Won in 10

October 7, 1961
vs. Alex Miteff
Freedom Hall
Louisville, Kentucky
Won, KO in 6

February 7, 1961
vs. Jim Robinson
Convention Hall
Miami Beach, Florida
Won, KO in 1

February 21, 1961
vs. Donnie Fleeman
Auditorium
Miami Beach, Florida
Won, KO in 7

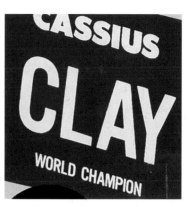

April 19, 1961
vs. Lamar Clark
Freedom Hall
Louisville, Kentucky
Won, KO in 2

November 29, 1961
vs. Willi Besmanoff
Freedom Hall,
Louisville, Kentucky
Won, KO in 7

February 10, 1962
vs. Sonny Banks
Madison Square Garden
New York City
Won, KO in 4

February 29, 1962
vs. Don Warner
Convention Hall
Miami Beach, Florida
Won, KO in 4

The Fights

1962-1966

April 23, 1962
vs. George Logan
Memorial Sports Arena
Los Angeles, California
Won, KO in 4

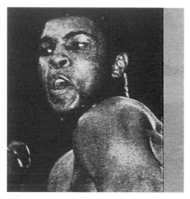

May 19, 1962
vs. Billy Daniels
St. Nicholas Arena
New York City
Won, KO in 7

July 20, 1962
vs. Alejandro Lavorante
Memorial Sports Arena
Los Angeles, California
Won, KO in 5

June 18, 1963
vs. Henry Cooper
Wembley Stadium
London, England
Won, KO in 5

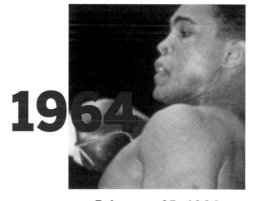

1964

February 25, 1964
vs. Sonny Liston
Convention Hall
Miami Beach, Florida
Won, KO in 7
WON HEAVYWEIGHT TITLE

1965

May 25, 1965
vs. Sonny Liston
St. Dominic's Arena
Lewiston, Maine
Won, KO in 1
RETAINED HEAVYWEIGHT TITLE

November 15, 1962
vs. Archie Moore
Memorial Sports Arena
Los Angeles, California
Won, KO in 4

1963

January 24, 1963
vs. Charlie Powell
Civic Arena
Pittsburgh, Pennsylvania
Won, KO in 3

March 13, 1963
vs. Doug Jones
Madison Square Garden
New York City
Won in 10

November 22, 1965
vs. Floyd Patterson
Convention Center
Las Vegas, Nevada
Won, KO in 12
RETAINED HEAVYWEIGHT TITLE

1966

March 29, 1966
vs. George Chuvalo
Maple Leaf Gardens
Toronto, Canada
Won in 15
RETAINED HEAVYWEIGHT TITLE

May 21, 1966
vs. Henry Cooper
Arsenal Stadium
London, England
Won, KO in 6
RETAINED HEAVYWEIGHT TITLE

1966-1971

August 6, 1966
vs. Brian London
Earls Court Stadium
London, England
Won, KO in 3
RETAINED HEAVYWEIGHT TITLE

September 10, 1966
vs. Karl Mildenberger
Wald Stadium
Frankfurt, Germany
Won, KO in 12
RETAINED HEAVYWEIGHT TITLE

November 14, 1966
vs. Cleveland Williams
Astrodome
Houston, Texas
Won, KO in 3
RETAINED HEAVYWEIGHT TITLE

October 26, 1970
vs. Jerry Quarry
Municipal Auditorium
Atlanta, Georgia
Won, KO in 3

December 7, 1970
vs. Oscar Bonavena
Madison Square Garden
New York City
Won, KO in 15

March 8, 1971
vs. Joe Frazier
Madison Square Garden,
New York City
Lost in 15
(FOR TITLE)

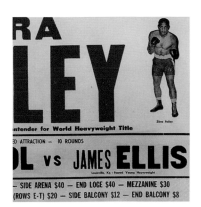

March 22, 1967

vs. Zora Folley

Madison Square Garden

New York City

Won, KO in 7

RETAINED HEAVYWEIGHT TITLE

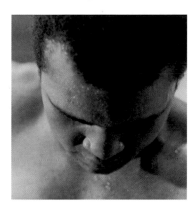

April 28, 1967-1970

Refuses induction

into the Army,

License suspended

November 17, 1971

vs. Buster Mathis

Astrodome

Houston, Texas

Won in 12

December 26, 1971

vs. Jurgen Blin

Hallenstadion Arena

Zurich, Switzerland

Won, KO in 7

1972-1974

April 1, 1972
vs. Mac Foster
Martial Arts Hall
Tokyo, Japan
Won in 15

May 1, 1972
vs. George Chu
Pacific Coliseum
Vancouver, Canada
Won in 15

February 14, 1973
vs. Joe Bugner
Convention Center
Las Vegas, Nevada
Won in 12

March 31, 1973
vs. Ken Norton
Sports Arena
San Diego, California
Lost in 12

July 19, 1972
vs. Al Lewis
Croke Park
Dublin, Ireland
Won, KO in 11

September 20, 1972
vs. Floyd Patterson
Madison Square Garden
New York City
Won, KO in 8

November 21, 1972
vs. Bob Foster
High Sierra Theatre
Stateline, Nevada
Won, KO in 8

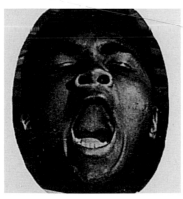

October 20, 1973
vs. Rudi Lubbers
Senyan Stadium
Djakarta, Indonesia
Won in 12

1974

January 28, 1974
vs. Joe Frazier
Madison Square Garden
New York City
Won in 12

October 30, 1974
vs. George Foreman
20th of May Stadium
Kinshasa, Zaire
Won, KO in 8
REGAINED HEAVYWEIGHT TITLE

1975-1978

1975

March 24, 1975
vs. Chuck Wepner
Coliseum
Cleveland, Ohio
Won, KO in 15
RETAINED HEAVYWEIGHT TITLE

May 16, 1975
vs. Ron Lyle
Convention Center
Las Vegas, Nevada
Won, KO in 11
RETAINED HEAVYWEIGHT TITLE

June 30, 1975
vs. Joe Bugner
Merdeka Stadium
Kuala Lumpur, Malaysia
Won in 15
RETAINED HEAVYWEIGHT TITLE

1977

May 24, 1976
vs. Richard Dunn
Olymphialle
Munich, Germany
Won, KO in 5
RETAINED HEAVYWEIGHT TITLE

September 28, 1976
vs. Ken Norton
Yankee Stadium
New York City
Won in 15
RETAINED HEAVYWEIGHT TITLE

May 16, 1977
vs. Alfredo Evangelista
Capital Center
Landover, Maryland
Won in 15
RETAINED HEAVYWEIGHT TITLE

October 1, 1975

vs. Joe Frazier

Araheta Coliseum

Quezon City, Philippines

Won, KO in 15

RETAINED HEAVYWEIGHT TITLE

1976

February 20, 1976

vs. Jean-Pierre Coopman

Clemente Coliseum

Hato Rey, Puerto Rico

Won, KO in 5

RETAINED HEAVYWEIGHT TITLE

April 30, 1976

vs. Jimmy Young

Capital Center,

Landover, Maryland

Won in 15

RETAINED HEAVYWEIGHT TITLE

1978

September 29, 1977

vs. Earnie Shavers

Madison Square Garden

New York City

Won in 15

RETAINED HEAVYWEIGHT TITLE

February 15, 1978

vs. Leon Spinks

Las Vegas Hilton

Las Vegas, Nevada

Lost in 15

(FOR TITLE)

September 15, 1978

vs. Leon Spinks

Superdome

New Orleans, Louisiana

Won in 15

REGAINED HEAVYWEIGHT TITLE

The Fights

1979-1981

1979

June 27, 1979

Announced retirement

1980

October 2, 1980

vs. Larry Holmes

Caesar's Palace

Las Vegas, Nevada

Lost, KO in 11

(FOR TITLE)

1981

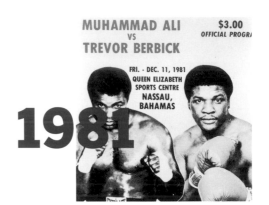

December 11, 1981

vs. Trevor Berbick

QEII Sports Centre

Nassau, Bahamas

Lost in 10

MUHAMMAD ALI CAREER RECORD

1960-1981

56 WINS (37 BY KNOCKOUT)

5 LOSSES (1 BY KNOCKOUT)

3 HEAVYWEIGHT TITLES

Contributors

James Earl Jones, the son of a prizefighter, starred as Malcolm X in *The Greatest*, a 1977 film adaptation of Muhammad Ali's life. During his three-decade career, Jones has starred in a wide variety of films, including *The Great White Hope, Cry The Beloved Country, Field of Dreams, Patriot Games, The River Niger*, and *Gardens of Stone*. He has lent his voice to numerous documentaries (*King, Malcolm X*) and to Darth Vadar in *Star Wars*.

Alex Haley is the author of *Roots: The Saga of an American Family* and *The Autobiography of Malcolm X*. In 1964, Haley, an interviewer for *Playboy* magazine, talked with the young Cassius Clay, who fresh off a stunning upset of Sonny Liston, had been crowned the new heavyweight champion. The interview was wide-ranging, covering everything from Liston to Malcolm X, from the temptations of women to Clay's "terrible" poetry.

Norman Mailer is the Pulitzer Prize-winning author of *The Naked and the Dead, Advertisements for Myself, The Executioner's Song* and *Harlot's Ghost*. Despite the enormous popularity of these and other of his books, many think his most impassioned tome is *The Fight*, a 1975 recounting of his trip as a reporter to the heart of Africa to cover "The Rumble in the Jungle," the legendary Ali-Foreman heavyweight bout.

Joyce Carol Oates is a prolific poet and novelist and the author of *On Boxing*, from which her essay on Ali is taken. In the foreword of *On Boxing*, Oates states that "No other subject is, for the writer, so intensely personal as boxing.... To write about boxing is to be forced to contemplate not only boxing, but the perimeters of civilization—what it is, or should be, to be 'human.'"

Peter Richmond is a special correspondent for *GQ*, where "Muhammad in Excelsis" originally appeared. It was included in a 1998 special issue focusing on Ali entitled "The Athlete of the Century."

Neil Leifer photographed Ali throughout his career, beginning with a 1965 shoot where a young Clay met him skeptically: "You're just a kid; you sure you know what you're doing?" But Leifer won him over: "I handed him the Polaroid, and he studied it very carefully. A big smile crossed his face as he waved the snapshot....'Hmmm, not bad! Boy, ain't I pretty? OK, maybe you know what you're doing.' He took another look at the Polaroid and pointed to himself. 'But how can you miss with a subject like me?'"

Credits

Introduction ©1999 by James Earl Jones.

1960s Alex Haley piece originally appeared in *Playboy* magazine as "The *Playboy* Interview: Cassius Clay." Reproduced by special permission of *Playboy* magazine. Copyright ©1964 by *Playboy*. All rights reserved.

1970s Norman Mailer piece from *The Fight* by Norman Mailer, ©1975 by Norman Mailer. Reprinted by permission of The Wylie Agency.

1980s Joyce Carol Oates piece from *On Boxing* by Joyce Carol Oates, ©1987, 1995 by the Ontario Review. Reprinted by permission of the author.

1990s Peter Richmond piece "Muhammad in Excelsis" courtesy of *GQ*. 1998 by Condé Nast Publications, Inc. Reprinted by permission of Condé Nast Publications, Inc.

Quotes used throughout are from the following sources:

"Muhammad Ali Challenges Black Men" by Charles L. Sanders from *Ebony* magazine, January 1975.

"The *Playboy* Interview: Muhammad Ali" from *Playboy*, November 1975.

"Ali: Still Magic" by Peter Tauber from *The New York Times Magazine*, July 17, 1988.

"An Intimate Look at a Legend" by Hans J. Massouri from *Ebony* magazine, November 1989.

Muhammad Ali: His Life and Times by Thomas Hauser, Random House, 1991.

"Young Cassius" from *Sports Illustrated*, January 13, 1992.

"Lawdy, Lawdy, He's Great" by Mark Kram from *Sports Illustrated*, October 3, 1994.

Muhammad Ali by John Stravinsky, Random House, 1997.

"The World's Champion" by William Plummer from *People* magazine, January 13, 1997.

King of the World by David Remnick, Random House, 1998.

The Muhammad Ali Reader, edited by Gerald Early, Ecco Press, 1998.

"The Child of the Sixties," by Wilfred Sheed, from *GQ* special issue "The Athlete of the Century," April 1998.

All fight posters and memorabilia and photograph on page 6 ©Christie's Images. Used by permission of Christie's Images.

Photographs on page 13, 26, 31, 35, 43, 45, 49, 57, 68, 70, 71, 90, 97, 99, 106 ©Neil Leifer. Used by permission of the photographer.

Photographs on page 7, 17, 24, 28 (left), 29, 40, 46, 54, 82, 85, 88, 89, 92, 94, 117, 118, 119, 120, 121, 124, 125, 126, 127 ©UPI/Corbis-Bettmann. Used by permission of UPI/Corbis-Bettmann.

Photographs on page 5, 27, 28 (right), 51, 61, 105, 112, 116, 120, 123 ©Archive Photos. Used by permission of Archive Photos.

Photographs on page 103, 114 ©PNI. Used by permission of PNI.

IONAL

EATRE

ED STS.

Inc.

NTLEY

5 Rounds

IONSHIP

IE

ELL

K SEAT

TUES. EVE.

MARCH 29 1966

MUHAMMAD ALI vs ERNIE TERRELL

BOX

71A

BOX SEA

$50.00

ES. EVE.

ARCH

— 8:30 P. M.

29

INTERNAT
AMPHITH

42nd & HALS

NATIONAL SPORTS PROMOTION

IRV. SCHOENWALD AND BEN BE

PRESENT

orld Heavyweight Championship - 1

FOR UNDISPUTED WORLD HEAVYWEIGHT CHAM

MUHAMMAD
ALI

VS

ER
TER

50.00

Est. Price $45.45

State Tax $4.55

BO